NIST Special Publication 800-55 Revision 1

Performance Measurement Guide for Information Security

National Institute of Standards and Technology
U.S. Department of Commerce

Elizabeth Chew, Marianne Swanson, Kevin Stine, Nadya Bartol, Anthony Brown, and Will Robinson

INFORMATION SECURITY

Computer Security Division
Information Technology Laboratory
National Institute of Standards and Technology
Gaithersburg, MD 20899-8930

July 2008

U.S. Department of Commerce
Carlos M. Gutierrez, Secretary

National Institute of Standards and Technology
James M. Turner, Deputy Director

Reports on Computer Systems Technology

The Information Technology Laboratory (ITL) at the National Institute of Standards and Technology (NIST) promotes the U.S. economy and public welfare by providing technical leadership for the Nation's measurement and standards infrastructure. ITL develops tests, test methods, reference data, proof of concept implementations, and technical analyses to advance the development and productive use of information technology. ITL's responsibilities include the development of management, administrative, technical, and physical standards and guidelines for the cost-effective security and privacy of sensitive unclassified information in federal computer systems. This Special Publication 800-series reports on ITL's research, guidelines, and outreach efforts in information security, and its collaborative activities with industry, government, and academic organizations.

Authority

This document has been developed by the National Institute of Standards and Technology (NIST) in furtherance of its statutory responsibilities under the Federal Information Security Management Act (FISMA) of 2002, Public Law 107-347.

NIST is responsible for developing standards and guidelines, including minimum requirements, and for providing adequate information security for all agency operations and assets, but such standards and guidelines shall not apply to national security systems. This guideline is consistent with the requirements of the Office of Management and Budget (OMB) Circular A-130, Section 8b(3), *Securing Agency Information Systems*, as analyzed in A-130, Appendix IV: *Analysis of Key Sections*. Supplemental information is provided in A-130, Appendix III.

This guideline has been prepared for use by federal agencies. It may also be used by nongovernmental organizations on a voluntary basis and is not subject to copyright regulations. (Attribution would be appreciated by NIST.)

Nothing in this document should be taken to contradict standards and guidelines made mandatory and binding on federal agencies by the Secretary of Commerce under statutory authority. Nor should these guidelines be interpreted as altering or superseding the existing authorities of the Secretary of Commerce, Director of the OMB, or any other federal official.

Certain commercial entities, equipment, or materials may be identified in this document in order to describe an experimental procedure or concept adequately. Such identification is not intended to imply recommendation or endorsement by NIST, nor is it intended to imply that the entities, materials, or equipment are necessarily the best available for the purpose.

Acknowledgements

The authors wish to thank Joan Hash (NIST), Arnold Johnson (NIST), Elizabeth Lennon (NIST), Karen Scarfone (NIST), Kelley Dempsey (NIST), and Karen Quigg (MITRE) who reviewed drafts of this document and/or contributed to its development. The authors also gratefully acknowledge and appreciate the many contributions from individuals and organizations in the public and private sectors whose thoughtful and constructive comments improved the quality and usefulness of this publication.

TABLE OF CONTENTS

EXECUTIVE SUMMARY .... **VIII**

1. INTRODUCTION 1
    1.1 Purpose and Scope 1
    1.2 Audience 2
    1.3 History 2
    1.4 Critical Success Factors 3
    1.5 Relationship to Other NIST Documents 4
    1.6 Document Organization 5

2. ROLES AND RESPONSIBILITIES 6
    2.1 Agency Head 6
    2.2 Chief Information Officer 6
    2.3 Senior Agency Information Security Officer 7
    2.4 Program Manager/Information System Owner 8
    2.5 Information System Security Officer 8
    2.6 Other Related Roles 8

3. INFORMATION SECURITY MEASURES BACKGROUND 9
    3.1 Definition 9
    3.2 Benefits of Using Measures 10
    3.3 Types of Measures 11
        3.3.1 Implementation Measures 13
        3.3.2 Effectiveness/Efficiency Measures 13
        3.3.3 Impact Measures 14
    3.4 Measurement Considerations 15
        3.4.1 Organizational Considerations 15
        3.4.2 Manageability 15
        3.4.3 Data Management Concerns 16
        3.4.4 Automation of Measurement Data Collection 16
    3.5 Information Security Measurement Program Scope 17
        3.5.1 Individual Information Systems 17
        3.5.2 System Development Life Cycle 17
        3.5.3 Enterprise-Wide Programs 19

4. LEGISLATIVE AND STRATEGIC DRIVERS 20
    4.1 Legislative Considerations 20
        4.1.1 Government Performance Results Act 20
        4.1.2 Federal Information Security Management Act 21
    4.2 Federal Enterprise Architecture 22
    4.3 Linkage Between Enterprise Strategic Planning and Information Security .. 23

5. MEASURES DEVELOPMENT PROCESS 24
    5.1 Stakeholder Interest Identification 25

5.2	Goals and Objectives Definition	26
5.3	Information Security Policies, Guidelines, and Procedures Review	27
5.4	Information Security Program Implementation Review	27
5.5	Measures Development and Selection	28
5.5.1	Measures Development Approach	29
5.5.2	Measures Prioritization and Selection	29
5.5.3	Establishing Performance Targets	30
5.6	Measures Development Template	31
5.7	Feedback Within the Measures Development Process	33
6.	**INFORMATION SECURITY MEASUREMENT IMPLEMENTATION**	**35**
6.1	Prepare for Data Collection	35
6.2	Collect Data and Analyze Results	36
6.3	Identify Corrective Actions	38
6.4	Develop Business Case and Obtain Resources	38
6.5	Apply Corrective Actions	40

APPENDIX A: CANDIDATE MEASURES **A-1**

APPENDIX B: ACRONYMS **B-1**

APPENDIX C: REFERENCES **C-1**

APPENDIX D: SPECIFICATIONS FOR MINIMUM SECURITY REQUIREMENTS . D-1

LIST OF FIGURES

Figure 1-1. Information Security Measurement Program Structure 3
Figure 3-1. Information Security Program Maturity and Types of Measurement.........................12
Figure 5-1. Information Security Measures Development Process 25
Figure 5-2. Information Security Measures Trend Example 31
Figure 6-1. Information Security Measurement Program Implementation Process 35

LIST OF TABLES

Table 1. Measurement During System Development 18
Table 2. Measures Template and Instructions 32

EXECUTIVE SUMMARY

This document is a guide to assist in the development, selection, and implementation of measures to be used at the information system and program levels. These measures indicate the effectiveness of security controls applied to information systems and supporting information security programs. Such measures are used to facilitate decision making, improve performance, and increase accountability through the collection, analysis, and reporting of relevant performance-related data—providing a way to tie the implementation, efficiency, and effectiveness of information system and program security controls to an agency's success in achieving its mission. The performance measures development process described in this guide will assist agency information security practitioners in establishing a relationship between information system and program security activities under their purview and the agency mission, helping to demonstrate the value of information security to their organization.

A number of existing laws, rules, and regulations—including the Clinger-Cohen Act, the Government Performance and Results Act (GPRA), the Government Paperwork Elimination Act (GPEA), and the Federal Information Security Management Act (FISMA)—cite information performance measurement in general, and information security performance measurement in particular, as a requirement. In addition to legislative compliance, agencies can use performance measures as management tools in their internal improvement efforts and link implementation of their information security programs to agency-level strategic planning efforts.

The following factors must be considered during development and implementation of an information security measurement program:

- Measures must yield quantifiable information (percentages, averages, and numbers);

- Data that supports the measures needs to be readily obtainable;

- Only repeatable information security processes should be considered for measurement; and

- Measures must be useful for tracking performance and directing resources.

The measures development process described in this document ensures that measures are developed with the purpose of identifying causes of poor performance and pointing to appropriate corrective actions.

This document focuses on the development and collection of three types of measures:

- Implementation measures to measure execution of security policy;

- Effectiveness/efficiency measures to measure results of security services delivery; and

- Impact measures to measure business or mission consequences of security events.

The types of measures that can realistically be obtained, and that can also be useful for performance improvement, depend on the maturity of the agency's information security program and the information system's security control implementation. Although different types of measures can be used simultaneously, the primary focus of information security measures shifts as the implementation of security controls matures.

1. INTRODUCTION

The requirement to measure information security performance is driven by regulatory, financial, and organizational reasons. A number of existing laws, rules, and regulations cite information performance measurement in general, and information security performance measurement in particular, as a requirement. These laws include the Clinger-Cohen Act, the Government Performance and Results Act (GPRA), the Government Paperwork Elimination Act (GPEA), and the Federal Information Security Management Act (FISMA).

While these laws, rules, and regulations are important drivers for information security measurement, equally compelling are the benefits that information security performance measurement can yield for organizations. Agencies can use performance measures as management tools in their internal improvement efforts and link implementation of their information security programs to agency-level strategic planning efforts. Information security measures are used to facilitate decision making and improve performance and accountability through collection, analysis, and reporting of relevant performance-related data. They provide the means for tying the implementation, efficiency, and effectiveness of security controls to an agency's success in its mission-critical activities. The performance measures development process described in this document will assist agency information security practitioners in establishing a relationship between information system and program security activities under their purview and the agency mission, helping to demonstrate the value of information security to their organization.

1.1 Purpose and Scope

This document is a guide for the specific development, selection, and implementation of information system-level and program-level measures to indicate the implementation, efficiency/effectiveness, and impact of security controls, and other security-related activities. It provides guidelines on how an organization, through the use of measures, identifies the adequacy of in-place security controls, policies, and procedures. It provides an approach to help management decide where to invest in additional information security resources, identify and evaluate nonproductive security controls, and prioritize security controls for continuous monitoring. It explains the measurement development and implementation processes and how measures can be used to adequately justify information security investments and support risk-based decisions. The results of an effective information security measurement program can provide useful data for directing the allocation of information security resources and should simplify the preparation of performance-related reports. Successful implementation of such a program assists agencies in meeting the annual requirements of the Office of Management and Budget (OMB) to report the status of agency information security programs.

NIST Special Publication (SP) 800-55, Revision 1, expands upon NIST's previous work in the field of information security measures to provide additional program-level guidelines for quantifying information security performance in support of organizational strategic goals. The processes and methodologies described in this document link information system security performance to agency performance by leveraging agency-level strategic planning processes. By doing so, the processes and methodologies help demonstrate how information security contributes to accomplishing agency strategic goals and objectives. Performance measures developed according to this guide will enhance the ability of agencies to respond to a variety of federal government mandates and initiatives, including FISMA.

This publication uses the security controls identified in NIST SP 800-53, *Recommended Security Controls for Federal Information Systems*, as a basis for developing measures that support the evaluation of information security programs. In addition to providing guidelines on developing measures, the guide lists a number of candidate measures that agencies can tailor, expand, or use as models for developing other measures.[1] While focused on NIST SP 800-53 security controls, the process described in this guide can be applied to develop agency-specific measures related to security controls that are not included in NIST SP 800-53.

The information security measurement program described in this document can be helpful in fulfilling regulatory requirements. The program provides an underlying data collection, analysis, and reporting infrastructure that can be tailored to support FISMA performance measures, Federal Enterprise Architecture's (FEA) Performance Reference Model (PRM) requirements, and any other enterprise-specific requirements for reporting quantifiable information about information security performance.

1.2   Audience

This guide is written primarily for Chief Information Officers (CIOs), Senior Agency Information Security Officers (SAISOs)—often referred to as Chief Information Security Officers (CISOs)—and Information System Security Officers (ISSOs). It targets individuals who are familiar with security controls as described in NIST SP 800-53. The concepts, processes, and candidate measures presented in this guide can be used within government and industry contexts.

1.3   History

The approach for measuring security control effectiveness has been under development for several years. NIST SP 800-55, *Security Metrics Guide for Information Technology Systems*, and NIST Draft SP 800-80, *Guide to Developing Performance Metrics for Information Security,* both addressed information security measurement. This document supersedes these publications by building upon them to align this approach with security controls provided in NIST SP 800-53, *Recommended Security Controls for Federal Information Systems*. The document also expands on concepts and processes introduced in the original version of NIST SP 800-55 to assist with the assessment of information security program implementation.

Security control implementation for information systems and information security programs is reviewed and reported annually to OMB in accordance with the Electronic Government Act of 2002, which includes FISMA. The Act requires departments and agencies to demonstrate that

---

[1] Candidate measures offered by this guide do not constitute mandatory requirements. Rather, they provide a sampling of measures to be considered for use by the readers of this guide.

they are meeting applicable information security requirements, and to document the level of performance based on results of annual program reviews.

1.4 Critical Success Factors

An information security measurement program within an organization should include four interdependent components (see Figure 1-1).

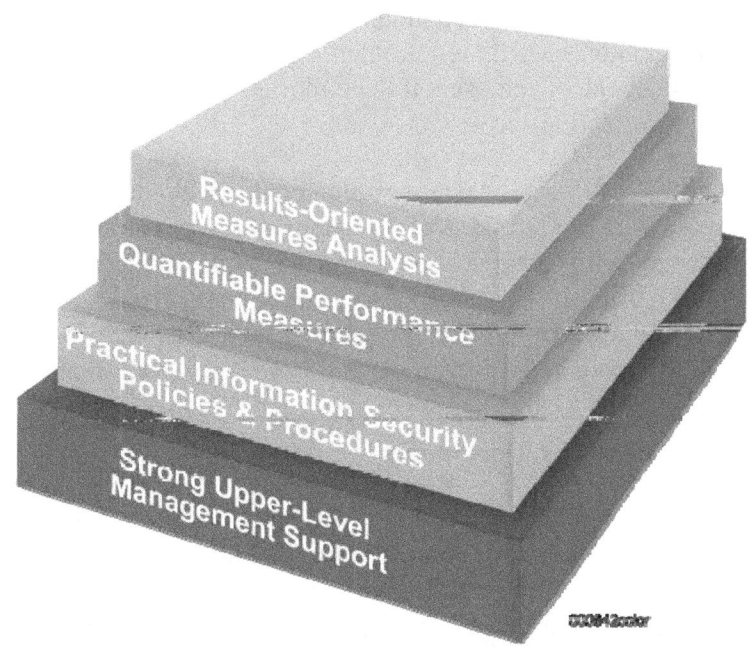

Figure 1-1. Information Security Measurement Program Structure

The foundation of strong upper-level management support is critical, not only for the success of the information security program, but also for the program's implementation. This support establishes a focus on information security within the highest levels of the organization. Without a solid foundation (i.e., proactive support of personnel in positions that control information resources), the information security measurement program can fail when pressured by organizational dynamics and budget limitations.

The second component of an effective information security measurement program is the existence of information security policies and procedures backed by the authority necessary to enforce compliance. Information security policies delineate the information security management structure, clearly assign information security responsibilities, and lay the foundation needed to reliably measure progress and compliance. Procedures document management's position on the implementation of an information security control and the rigor with which it is applied. Measures are not easily obtainable if no procedures are in place that supply data to be used for measurement.

The third component is developing and establishing quantifiable performance measures that are designed to capture and provide meaningful performance data. To provide meaningful data, quantifiable information security measures must be based on information security performance goals and objectives, and be easily obtainable and feasible to measure. They must also be repeatable, provide relevant performance trends over time, and be useful for tracking performance and directing resources.

Finally, the information security measurement program itself must emphasize consistent periodic analysis of the measures data. Results of this analysis are used to apply lessons learned, improve effectiveness of existing security controls, and plan for the implementation of future security controls to meet new information security requirements as they occur. Accurate data collection must be a priority with stakeholders and users if the collected data is to be meaningful and useful in improving the overall information security program.

The success of an information security program implementation should be judged by the degree to which meaningful results are produced. A comprehensive information security measurement program should provide substantive justification for decisions that directly affect the information security posture of an organization. These decisions include budget and personnel requests and allocation of available resources. An information security measurement program should assist in the preparation of required reports relating to information security performance.

1.5 Relationship to Other NIST Documents

This document is a continuation in a series of NIST special publications intended to assist information management and information security personnel in the establishment, implementation, and maintenance of an information security program. It focuses on quantifying information security performance based on the results of a variety of information security activities. This approach draws upon many sources of data, including:

- Information security assessment and testing efforts such as those described in NIST SP 800-53A, *Guide for Assessing the Security Controls in Federal Information Systems;*
- Information security risk assessments efforts, such as those described in NIST SP 800-30, *Risk Management Guide for Information Technology Systems*; and
- Minimum security controls recommended in NIST SP 800-53, *Recommended Security Controls for Federal Information Systems*.

NIST SP 800-55, Revision 1, differs from NIST SP 800-53A in that it provides a quantitative approach to measuring and analyzing security controls implementation and effectiveness at the information system and program levels, aggregated across multiple individual efforts. It also provides an approach for aggregating information from multiple information systems to measure and analyze information security from an enterprise-level perspective. NIST SP 800-53A provides procedures for assessing if the security controls are implemented and operating as intended according to the information system security plan for the system. The assessment data produced as a result of applying NIST SP 800-53A assessment procedures can serve as a data source for information security measurement.

Information security measurement results described in this guide will provide inputs into the information security program activities described in a number of NIST publications, including:

- NIST SP 800-100, *Information Security Handbook: A Guide for Managers*; and

- NIST SP 800-65, *Integrating IT Security into the Capital Planning and Investment Control Process*.

These measures can also be used to assist with prioritization for the continuous monitoring of security controls, as described in NIST SP 800-37, *Guide for the Security Certification and Accreditation of Federal Information Systems*.

1.6 Document Organization

The remaining sections of this guide discuss the following:

- Section 2, Roles and Responsibilities, describes the roles and responsibilities of agency staff that have a direct interest in the success of the information security program, and in the establishment of an information security measurement program.

- Section 3, Information Security Measures Background, provides guidelines on the background and definition of information security measures, the benefits of implementation, various types of information security measures, and the factors that directly affect success of an information security measurement program.

- Section 4, Legislative and Strategic Drivers, links information security to strategic planning through relevant legislation and guidelines.

- Section 5, Measures Development Process, presents the approach and process used for development of information security measures.

- Section 6, Information Security Measurement Implementation, discusses those factors that can affect the implementation of an information security measurement program.

This guide contains four appendices. Appendix A, Candidate Measures, provides practical examples of information security measures that can be used or modified to meet specific agency requirements. Appendix B provides a list of acronyms used in this document. Appendix C lists references. Appendix D lists specifications for minimum security requirements taken from Federal Information Processing Standard (FIPS) 200, *Minimum Security Requirements for Federal Information and Information Systems*.

2. ROLES AND RESPONSIBILITIES

This section outlines the key roles and responsibilities for developing and implementing information security measures. While information security is the responsibility of all members of the organization, the positions described in Sections 2.1 through 2.6 are key information security stakeholders that should work to instill a culture of information security awareness across the organization..

2.1 Agency Head

The specific Agency Head responsibilities related to information security measurement are as follows:

- Ensuring that information security measures are used in support of agency strategic and operational planning processes to secure the organization's mission;
- Ensuring that information security measures are integrated into annual reporting on the effectiveness of the agency information security program by the Chief Information Officer (CIO);
- Demonstrating support for information security measures development and implementation, and communicating official support to the agency;
- Ensuring that information security measurement activities have adequate financial and human resources for success;
- Actively promoting information security measurement as an essential facilitator of information security performance improvement throughout the agency; and
- Approving policy to officially institute measures collection.

2.2 Chief Information Officer [2]

The Chief Information Officer (CIO) has the following responsibilities related to information security measurement:

- Using information security measures to assist in monitoring compliance with applicable information security requirements;
- Using information security measures in annually reporting on effectiveness of the agency information security program to the agency head;
- Demonstrating management's commitment to information security measures development and implementation through formal leadership;

---

[2] When an agency has not designated a formal Chief Information Officer position, FISMA requires the associated responsibilities to be handled by a comparable agency official.

- Formally communicating the importance of using information security measures to monitor the overall health of the information security program and to comply with applicable regulations;

- Ensuring information security measurement program development and implementation;

- Allocating adequate financial and human resources to the information security measurement program;

- Reviewing information security measures regularly and using information security measures data to support policy, resource allocation, budget decisions, and assessment of the information security program posture and operational risks to agency information systems;

- Ensuring that a process is in place to address issues discovered through measures analysis and taking corrective actions such as revising information security procedures and providing additional information security training to staff; and

- Issuing policy, procedures, and guidelines to officially develop, implement, and institute measures.

2.3 Senior Agency Information Security Officer

Depending upon the agency, the Senior Agency Information Security Officer (SAISO) may sometimes be referred to as the Chief Information Security Officer (CISO). Within this document, the term SAISO is used to represent both the SAISO and the CISO. The SAISO has the following responsibilities related to information security measurement:

- Integrating information security measurement into the process for planning, implementing, evaluating, and documenting remedial actions to address any deficiencies in the information security policies, procedures, and practices of the agency;

- Obtaining adequate financial and human resources to support information security measurement program development and implementation;

- Leading the development of any internal guidelines or policy related to information security measures;

- Using information security measures in support of the agency CIO's annual reporting to the agency head on the effectiveness of the agency's information security program, including progress of remedial actions;

- Conducting information security measures development and implementation;

- Ensuring that a standard process is used throughout the agency for information security measures development, creation, analysis, and reporting; and,

- Using information security measures for policy, resource allocation, and budget decisions.

2.4 Program Manager/Information System Owner

Program managers, as well as information system owners, are responsible for ensuring that proper security controls are in place to address the confidentiality, integrity, and availability of information and information systems. The program manager/information system owner has the following responsibilities related to information security measurement:

- Participating in information security measurement program development and implementation by providing feedback on the feasibility of data collection and identifying data sources and repositories;

- Educating staff on the development, collection, analysis, and reporting of information security measures and how it will affect information security policy, requirements, resource allocation, and budget decisions;

- Ensuring that measurement data is collected consistently and accurately and is provided to designated staff who are analyzing and reporting the data;

- Directing full participation and cooperation of staff, when required;

- Reviewing information security measures data regularly and using it for policy, resource allocation, and budget decisions; and

- Supporting implementation of corrective actions, identified through measuring information security performance.

2.5 Information System Security Officer

The Information System Security Officer (ISSO) has the following responsibilities related to information security measurement:

- Participating in information security measurement program development and implementation by providing feedback on the feasibility of data collection and identifying data sources and repositories; and

- Collecting data or providing measurement data to designated staff that are collecting, analyzing, and reporting the data.

2.6 Other Related Roles

Information security measurement may require inputs from a variety of organizational components or stakeholders, including incident response, information technology operations, privacy, enterprise architecture, human resources, physical security, and others. Section 5.1 lists additional stakeholders.

3. INFORMATION SECURITY MEASURES BACKGROUND

This section provides basic information on what information security measures are and why information security performance should be measured. Additionally, this section defines types of measures that can be used; discusses the key aspects of making an information security measurement program successful; and identifies the uses of measures for management, reporting, and decision making.

3.1 Definition

Information security measures are used to facilitate decision making and improve performance and accountability through the collection, analysis, and reporting of relevant performance-related data. The purpose of measuring performance is to monitor the status of measured activities and facilitate improvement in those activities by applying corrective actions based on observed measurements.

Information security measures can be obtained at different levels within an organization. Detailed measures, collected at the information system level, can be aggregated and rolled up to progressively higher levels, depending on the size and complexity of an organization. While a case can be made for using different terms for more detailed and aggregated items, such as "metrics" and "measures," this document standardizes on "measures" to mean the results of data collection, analysis, and reporting. This document refers to the process of data collection, analysis, and reporting as "measurement."

Information security measures are based on information security performance goals and objectives. Information security performance goals state the desired results of an information or security program implementation, such as, "All employees should receive adequate information security awareness training." Information security performance objectives enable accomplishment of goals by identifying practices defined by information security policies and procedures that direct consistent implementation of security controls across the organization. Examples of information security performance objectives, corresponding to the example goal cited above, are: All new employees receive new employee training. Employee training includes a summary of the Rules of Behavior. Employee training includes a summary of, and a reference to, the organization's information security policies and procedures.

Information security measures monitor the accomplishment of goals and objectives by quantifying the implementation, efficiency, and effectiveness of security controls; analyzing the adequacy of information security program activities; and identifying possible improvement actions. During measures development, goals and objectives from federal guidelines, legislation, regulations, and enterprise-level guidance are identified and prioritized to ensure that the measurable aspects of information security performance correspond to the operational priorities of the organization.

Information security measures must yield quantifiable information for comparison purposes, apply formulas for analysis, and track changes using the same points of reference. Percentages or averages are most common. Absolute numbers are sometimes useful, depending on the activity that is being measured.

Data required for calculating measures must be readily obtainable, and the process that is under consideration needs to be measurable. Only processes that can be consistent and repeatable should be considered for measurement. Even though the processes may be repeatable and stable, measurable data may be difficult to obtain if the processes and their performance have not been documented. Measures must use easily obtainable data to ensure that the burden of measurement on the organization does not defeat the purpose of measurement by absorbing resources that may be needed elsewhere. Examples of information security activities that can provide data for measurement include risk assessments, penetration testing, security assessments, and continuous monitoring. Other assessment activities (such as the effectiveness of a training and awareness program) can also be quantified and used as data sources for measures.

To be useful in tracking performance and directing resources, measures need to provide relevant performance trends over time and point to improvement actions that can be applied to problem areas. Management should use measures to review performance by observing trends, identifying and prioritizing corrective actions, and directing the application of those corrective actions based on risk mitigation factors and available resources. The measures development process, described in Section 5, ensures that measures are developed with the purpose of identifying causes of poor performance and point to appropriate corrective actions.

3.2 Benefits of Using Measures

An information security measurement program provides a number of organizational and financial benefits. Major benefits include increasing accountability for information security performance; improving effectiveness of information security activities; demonstrating compliance with laws, rules and regulations; and providing quantifiable inputs for resource allocation decisions.

Increase Accountability: Information security measures can increase accountability for information security by helping to identify specific security controls that are implemented incorrectly, are not implemented, or are ineffective. Data collection and analysis processes can facilitate identification of the personnel responsible for security controls implementation within specific organizational components or for specific information systems.

Improve Information Security Effectiveness: An information security measurement program will enable organizations to quantify improvements in securing information systems and demonstrate quantifiable progress in accomplishing agency strategic goals and objectives. Information security measures can assist with determining the effectiveness of implemented information security processes, procedures, and security controls by relating results of information security activities and events (e.g., incident data, revenue lost to cyber attacks) to security controls and information security investments.

Demonstrate Compliance: Organizations can demonstrate compliance with applicable laws, rules, and regulations by implementing and maintaining an information security measurement program. Information security measures will assist in satisfying the annual FISMA reporting requirement to state performance measures for past and current fiscal years. Additionally, information security measures can be used as input into the Government Accountability Office (GAO) and Inspectors General (IG) audits. Implementation of an information security measurement program will demonstrate agency commitment to proactive information security. It will also greatly reduce time spent by agencies in collecting data, which is routinely requested by the GAO and IG during audits and for subsequent status updates.

Provide Quantifiable Inputs for Resource Allocation Decisions: Fiscal constraints and market conditions compel government and industry to operate on reduced budgets. In such an environment, it is difficult to justify broad investments in the information security infrastructure. Information security investments should be allocated in accordance with a comprehensive risk management program. Use of information security measures will support risk-based decision making by contributing quantifiable information to the risk management process. It will allow organizations to measure successes and failures of past and current information security investments, and should provide quantifiable data that will support resource allocation for future investments. Using the results of the measures analysis, program managers and system owners can isolate problems, use collected data to justify investment requests, and then target investments specifically to the areas in need of improvement. By using measures to target security investments, these measures can aid organizations in obtaining the best value from available resources.

3.3 Types of Measures

The maturity of an organization's information security program determines the type of measures that can be gathered successfully. A program's maturity is defined by the existence and institutionalization of processes and procedures. As an information security program matures, its policies become more detailed and better documented, the processes it uses become more standardized and repeatable, and the program produces a greater quantity of data that can be used for performance measurement.

Figure 3-1 depicts this continuum by illustrating measurement considerations for information security programs. As Figure 3-1 illustrates, less mature information security programs need to develop their goals and objectives before being able to implement effective measurement. More mature programs use implementation measures to evaluate performance, while the most mature programs use effectiveness/efficiency and business impact measures to determine the effect of their information security processes and procedures.

An information security program is dependent upon upper-level management support to define its goals and objectives. These goals and objectives may be expressed through information security policies and processes at the program's inception, or in a variety of other sources. (Goals and objectives are addressed in more detail in Sections 4.1 and 5.2.) Information security policies are documented, and information security procedures begin to stabilize, as the program is implemented and begins to mature. To be useful, information security measurement requires existence of documented procedures and some available data on the implementation of security controls.

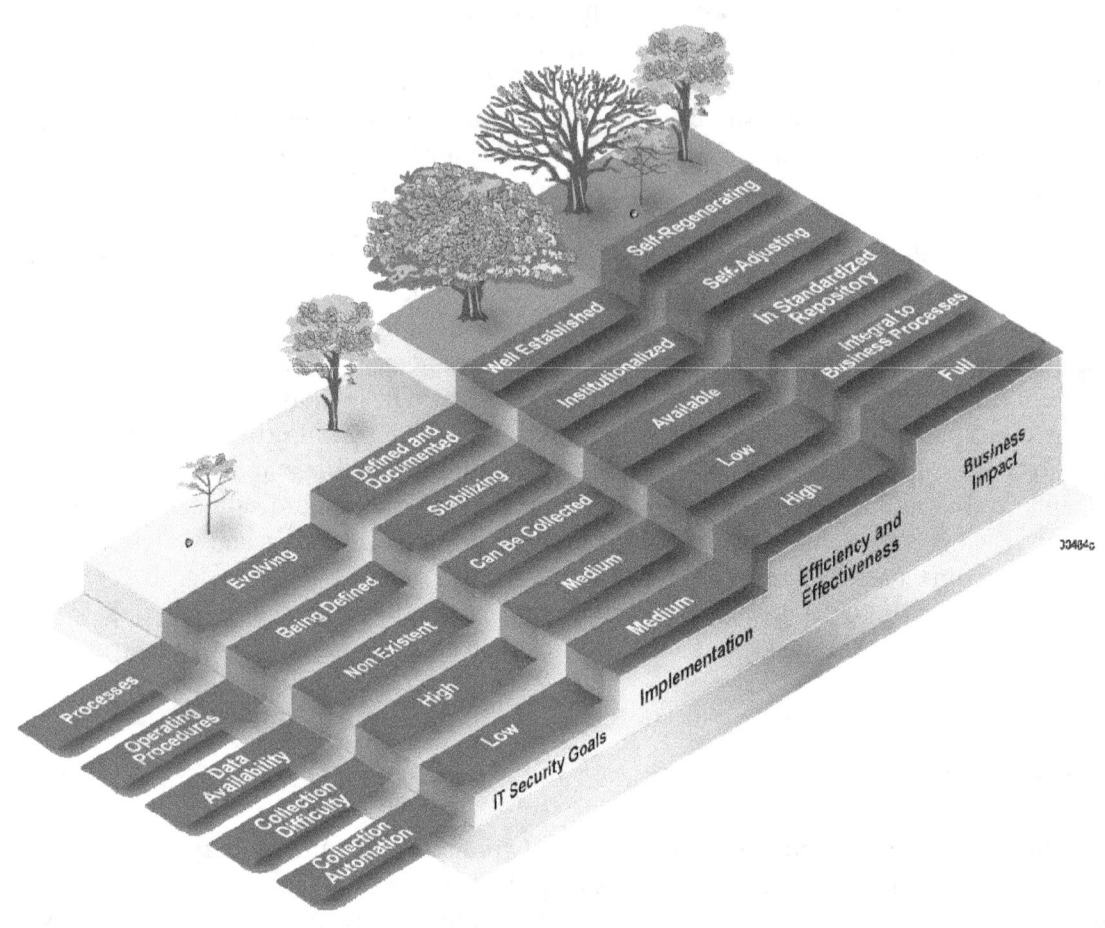

Figure 3-1. Information Security Program Maturity and Types of Measurement

A mature program normally uses multiple tracking mechanisms to document and quantify various aspects of its performance. As more data becomes available, the difficulty of measurement decreases and the ability to automate data collection increases. Data collection automation depends on the availability of data from automated sources versus the availability of data input by personnel. Manual data collection involves developing questionnaires and conducting interviews and surveys with the organization's staff. More usable data is available from semi automated and automated data sources—such as self-assessment tools, certification and accreditation (C&A) databases, and incident reporting/response databases—as an information security program matures. Measures data collection is considered to be fully automated when all data is gathered by automated data sources without human involvement or intervention.

Types of measures (implementation, effectiveness/efficiency, and impact) that can realistically be obtained and are useful for performance improvement depend on the maturity of the security control implementation. Although different types of measures can be used simultaneously, the primary focus of information security measures shifts as implementation of the information security program matures. As information security program goals and strategic plans are documented and implemented, the ability to reliably collect the outcome of their implementation improves. As an organization's information security program evolves and performance data becomes more readily available, measures will focus on program effectiveness/efficiency and the operational results of security control implementation. Once information security is integrated into an organization's processes, the processes become repeatable, measurement data collection becomes fully automated, and the mission or business impact of information security-related actions and events can be determined by analyzing and correlating the measurement data. Appendix A contains examples of implementation, effectiveness/efficiency, and impact measures.

3.3.1 Implementation Measures

Implementation measures are used to demonstrate progress in implementing information security programs, specific security controls, and associated policies and procedures. Examples of implementation measures related to information security programs include the *percentage of information systems with approved system security plans* and the *percentage of information systems with password policies configured as required*. At first, the results of these measures might be less than 100 percent. However, as the information security program and its associated policies and procedures mature, results should reach and remain at 100 percent. At this point, the organization should begin to focus its measurement efforts on effectiveness/efficiency and impact measures.

Implementation measures can also examine system-level areas—for example, the *percentage of servers within a system with a standard configuration*. At first, the results of this system-level measure will likely be less than 100 percent. When the implementation measure results reach and remain at 100 percent, it can be concluded that the information systems have fully implemented the security controls addressed by this measure, and measurement activities can refocus on other controls in need of improvement. After most implementation measures reach and remain at 100 percent, the organization should begin to focus its measurement efforts on effectiveness/efficiency and impact measures. Organizations should never fully retire implementation measures because they are effective at pointing out specific security controls that are in need of improvement; however, as an organization matures, the emphasis and resources of the measurement program should shift away from implementation and towards effectiveness/efficiency and impact measures.

Implementation measures require data that can be easily obtained from information security assessment reports, quarterly and annual FISMA reports, plans of action and milestones (POA&M), and other commonly used means of documenting and tracking information security program activities.

3.3.2 Effectiveness/Efficiency Measures

Effectiveness/efficiency measures are used to monitor if program-level processes and system-level security controls are implemented correctly, operating as intended, and meeting the desired outcome. These measures concentrate on the evidence and results of assessments and may require multiple data points quantifying the degree to which information security controls are implemented and the resulting effect(s) on the organization's information security posture. For example, the *percentage of enterprise operating system vulnerabilities for which patches have been applied or that have been otherwise mitigated* is both an implementation and effectiveness measure. It measures the implementation of the security control Flaw Remediation (SI-2) in SP 800-53 because the result of the measure demonstrates whether or not vulnerabilities are mitigated through patches or other means. At the same time, the result indicates the effectiveness of the Security Alerts and Advisories (SI-5) security control because any result less than the target indicates a lack of ability to receive alerts and use them to successfully mitigate vulnerabilities.

Effectiveness/efficiency measures address two aspects of security control implementation results: the robustness of the result itself, referred to as ***effectiveness***, and the timeliness of the result, referred to as ***efficiency***. For example, the **effectiveness**/efficiency measure—*percentage of information security incidents caused by improperly configured access controls*—relies on information regarding the implementation and ***effectiveness*** of the following security controls: Incident Monitoring (IR-5); Audit Monitoring, Analysis, and Reporting (AU-6); and Monitoring Configuration Changes (CM-4).

Additionally, the effectiveness/**efficiency** measure—*the percentage of system components that undergo maintenance on schedule*—relies on information regarding the ***efficiency*** of the following security controls: Periodic Maintenance (MA-2) and Life Cycle Support (SA-3).

Effectiveness/efficiency measures provide key information for information security decision makers about the results of previous policy and acquisition decisions. These measures can offer insight for improving performance of information security programs. Furthermore, effectiveness/efficiency measures can be used as a data source for continuous monitoring efforts because they help determine the effectiveness of security controls. The results of effectiveness/efficiency measures can be used to ascertain whether selected security controls are functioning properly and are helping facilitate corrective action prioritization.

Effectiveness/efficiency measures may require fusing information security program activities data with the data obtained from automated monitoring and evaluation tools in a manner that can be directly tied to security controls implementation.

3.3.3 Impact Measures

Impact measures are used to articulate the impact of information security on an organization's mission. These measures are inherently organization-specific since each organization has a unique mission. Depending upon the organization's mission, impact measures can be used to quantify:

- Cost savings produced by the information security program or through costs incurred from addressing information security events;

- The degree of public trust gained/maintained by the information security program; or

- Other mission-related impacts of information security.

These measures combine information about the results of security controls implementation with a variety of information about resources. They can provide the most direct insight into the value of information security to the organization and are the ones that are sought out by executives. For example, *the percentage of the agency's information system budget devoted to information security* relies on information regarding the implementation, effectiveness, and outcome of the following NIST SP 800-53 security controls: Allocation of Resources (SA-2) and Acquisitions (SA-4). Another, more generalized budget-related impact measure would be *the number of information security investments reported to OMB in an Exhibit 300.* Rather than examining the impact of a security control or controls, this measure evaluates the relationship between the portfolio of information security investments and the budget process.

Impact measures require tracking a variety of resource information across the organization in a manner that can be directly tied to information security activities and events.

3.4 Measurement Considerations

Organizations embarking on information security performance measurement should be aware of several considerations that can help make their program a success. These include specific organizational structure and processes as well as an understanding of required budget, personnel, and time resources.

3.4.1 Organizational Considerations

Appropriate stakeholders must be included in the development of information security measures and program implementation. Organizational elements that do not have information security as their primary responsibility but interact with information security on a regular basis (e.g., training, resource management, legal department) may need to be included in this process. (See Section 5.1 for more information on stakeholders.) If an organizational element exists that is responsible for performance measurement in general, the development and implementation of an information security measurement program should be coordinated with that organization. If a process exists for approving organization-wide data calls and actions, development and implementation of the information security measurement program should comply with the existing process.

3.4.2 Manageability

Any information security measurement program must be manageable for the implementing organization. Results of many information security activities can be quantified and used for performance measurement; however, since resources are limited and the majority of resources should be applied to correcting performance gaps, organizations should prioritize measurement requirements to ensure that a limited number of measures are gathered. Each stakeholder should be responsible for as few measures as possible—usually two to three measures per stakeholder. This helps ensure that the measures that are collected are meaningful, yield impact and outcome findings, and provide stakeholders with the time necessary to use the results to address performance gaps. As the program matures and target levels of measurement are reached, obsolete measures should be phased out and new ones that measure completion and effectiveness of more current items should be used. New measures will also be required if the organization's mission is redefined or if changes are made to information security policies and guidelines.

3.4.3 Data Management Concerns

To ascertain the quality and validity of data, data collection methods and data repositories used for measures data collection and reporting, either directly or as data sources, should be standardized. The validity of data is suspect if the primary data source is an incident-reporting database that stores only the information reported by a few organizational elements, or if reporting processes between organizations are inconsistent. The importance of standardizing reporting processes cannot be overemphasized. When organizations are developing and implementing processes that may serve as inputs into an information security measurement program, they must ensure that data gathering and reporting are clearly defined to facilitate the collection of valid data.

Organizations must understand that although they may collect substantial amounts of information security data, not all data will be useful for their information security measurement program at any given point in time. Any data collection specifically for the purpose of information security measures must be as nonintrusive as possible—and of maximum usefulness to ensure that available resources are used primarily to correct problems rather than collect data. Establishment of an information security measurement program will require a substantial investment to ensure that the program is implemented in a way that will maximize its benefits. Benefits of the program are expected to outweigh the costs of investing resources to maintain the program.

Finally, the information contained in information security data repositories represents a significant collection of operational and vulnerability data. Due to the sensitivity of this data, information security performance measurement data repositories need to be protected accordingly.

3.4.4 Automation of Measurement Data Collection

Efficient data management is facilitated by automating measurement data collection. Automating measurement data collection standardizes data collection and reporting, and helps institutionalize measurement activity by integrating it into business processes. In addition, automated data collection minimizes opportunities for human error, leading to greater accuracy of available data. Standardized collection and reporting can also increase data availability, as collections are likely to be housed in a centralized database or similar data repository.

As a complement to automating performance measurement, organizations should also consider how performance measurement automation can supplement other automated information security tasks. For example, Extensible Markup Language (XML)-formatted configuration checklists can allow organizations to use Commercial Off-The-Shelf (COTS), Government Off-The-Shelf (GOTS), or open-source tools to automatically check their information security configuration and map it to technical compliance requirements. While these checklists are primarily used for compliance with regulations such as FISMA, they can also be used to map specific technical control settings to the corresponding NIST SP 800-53 security controls, which can make the verification of compliance more consistent and efficient. For example, a checklist could examine the password strength settings on a system and report whether or not those settings meet requirements specified in NIST SP 800-53. The results of such automated data collection could provide dynamic updates to an agency's automated information security performance measures to indicate if information security targets are being achieved and where corrective actions and mitigation activities are required.

3.5 Information Security Measurement Program Scope

An information security measurement program can be scoped to a variety of environments and needs:

- Quantifying information system-level security performance for an operational information system;

- Quantifying the integration of information security into the system development life cycle (SDLC) during information system and software development processes; and

- Quantifying enterprise-wide information security performance.

Information security measures can be applied to organizational units, sites, or other organizational constructs. Organizations should carefully define the scope of their information security measurement program based on specific stakeholder needs, strategic goals and objectives, operating environments, risk priorities, and information security program maturity.

3.5.1 Individual Information Systems

Information security measurement can be applied at the information system level to provide quantifiable data regarding the implementation, effectiveness/efficiency, or impact of required or desired security controls. Information system owners can use measures to support the determination of the information system's security posture, demonstrate compliance with organizational requirements, and identify areas in need of improvement. Information security measurement can support certification and accreditation activities (e.g. risk assessments, information system security plans, and continuous monitoring), FISMA reporting activities, or capital planning activities.

3.5.2 System Development Life Cycle

Information security measurement should be used throughout the SDLC to monitor implementation of appropriate security controls. Formalized measurement of information security during the SDLC provides information to the project manager that is essential to understanding how well information security is integrated into the SDLC and to what degree vulnerabilities are being introduced into the information system. Different measures may be useful for different project activities. The following table provides examples of information security measures that can be used during the SDLC for a variety of project activities.

Table 1. Measurement During System Development[3]

SDLC Phase	Relevant Measures	Purpose	Value
Acquisition/Development	• Percentage of product defects that negatively impact the security posture of the system	• Identify software defects that may be exploited in the future	• Provides insight into the effectiveness of life cycle processes and information security training for developers • Indicates need for additional security controls in operations
Acquisition/Development	• Percentage of information security requirements (i.e., security controls implemented) that are mapped to design	• Determine if security requirements are being planned and implemented	• Provides insight into inclusion of information security requirements in early releases • Provides insight into complexity of information security implementation • Indicates short- and long-term need for additional security controls in operations
Acquisition/Development	• Number of entry points for a module (should be the minimum necessary)	• Fewer entry points reduces the amount of monitoring required	• Provides insight into possibility of inherent vulnerabilities and increased enterprise risk
Acquisition/Development	• Number of discovered defects that are known as software vulnerabilities (e.g., buffer overflows and cross-site scripting) • Number of deviations between design, code, and requirements • Number of defects and the area of the code in which they were found (it is a higher risk to have the defects between components, unit seams, or other interfaces) • Percent of discovered vulnerabilities that have been mitigated	• Proactively address security defects prior to testing and implementation	• Helps minimize development and maintenance rework costs

---

[3] These measures were developed in collaboration with Department of Homeland Security Software Assurance Program.

SDLC Phase	Relevant Measures	Purpose	Value
Acquisition/Development	• Cost/schedule variance in information security activities	• Monitor planning and implementation of security activities	• Provides insight into cost and schedule risks to project success • Increases accuracy in planning of future projects
Implementation/Assessment	• Percentage of modules that contain vulnerabilities • Percentage of failed security control requirements	• Identify software defects that may be exploited in the future	• Provides insight into risk of the system being exploited when implemented • Indicates need for additional security controls in operations

Collecting and analyzing these types of measures will help the project manager in the following manner:

- Determine if software defects that may impact information security are being identified early in the life cycle where they are more cost-effective to fix;
- Identify and remove potential vulnerabilities in software and develop more secure design practices;
- Identify and investigate trends that require corrective actions, such as training or revising poorly written and confusing procedures;
- Determine if the information system will comply with required security controls; and
- Track trends in information security risk throughout the SDLC.

Collecting, analyzing, and reporting appropriate security measures during the SDLC can be used to improve integration of information security into the information system development effort to increase the overall assurance that system security requirements are built in rather than added later.

3.5.3 Enterprise-Wide Programs

Information security measurement can be implemented on an enterprise-wide level to monitor the implementation, effectiveness/efficiency, and impact on the organization's information security activities. Enterprise-level measures may be derived by aggregating multiple information system-level measures or developed by using the entire enterprise as the scope.

For an enterprise-wide measurement to be effective, the organization must operate at a certain level of maturity to ensure that processes the measures depend upon are consistent, repeatable, and can ensure availability of data across the enterprise.

4. LEGISLATIVE AND STRATEGIC DRIVERS

This section explains the relationship between overall agency performance measures reporting and information security performance measures reporting, and provides agencies with guidelines on how to link these two activities to ensure that their information security program contributes to overall accomplishment of the agency mission, goals, and objectives. Sections 4.1 and 4.2 provide an overview of the Government Performance Results Act (GPRA), the Federal Information Security Management Act (FISMA), and the Federal Enterprise Architecture from a performance measurement point of view and describe their associated performance management requirements, while Section 4.3 discusses the linkage between enterprise strategic planning and information security.

4.1 Legislative Considerations

Legislation such as GPRA and FISMA, along with executive regulations, is driving an increased emphasis on managing, quantifying, and reporting agency performance. The purpose of these efforts is to facilitate the streamlining of U.S. government operations, improve efficiencies in delivering services, and demonstrate the value of these services to the public. Agencies are required to strategically plan their initiatives and make these plans and corresponding performance measures available to the public. The Executive Branch also develops initiatives that may require organizations to collect and report performance measures.

4.1.1 Government Performance Results Act

GPRA focuses on improving program effectiveness and efficiency by adequately articulating program goals and providing information on program performance. To structure and facilitate program improvement, it requires agencies to develop multiyear strategic plans and annually report their performance against these plans.

The purpose of GPRA is to:

- Improve the confidence of the American people in the capability of the federal government by systematically holding federal agencies accountable for achieving program results;

- Initiate program performance reform with a series of pilot projects in setting program goals, measuring program performance against those goals, and reporting publicly on their progress;

- Improve federal program effectiveness and public accountability by promoting a new focus on results, service quality, and customer satisfaction;

- Help federal managers improve service delivery by requiring that they plan for meeting program objectives, and by providing them with information about program results and service quality;

- Improve congressional decision making by providing more objective information on achieving statutory objectives and by reporting on the relative effectiveness and efficiency of federal programs and spending; and
- Improve internal management of the federal government.[4]

GPRA mandates agencies to conduct strategic and performance planning that culminates in annual submissions of strategic plans and performance measures reports. GPRA puts this planning in the context of the overall agency Capital Planning and Investment Control (CPIC) process by emphasizing "managing for results—what the program accomplishes and how well the accomplishments match with the program's purpose and objectives."[5]

As a part of their annual strategic and performance planning processes, agencies should:

- Define their long-term and annual goals and objectives;
- Set measurable targets of performance; and
- Report their performance against goals and objectives to the Office of Management and Budget (OMB) on a quarterly basis.

This performance measures reporting directly supports GPRA by providing a means to track performance against agency goals and objectives and measurable performance targets. Agencies can demonstrate the impact of information security on their missions by aligning information security performance measures with their information security goals and objectives.

GPRA is implemented by OMB Circular A-11, *Preparation, Submission, and Execution of the Budget, Part 6*.

4.1.2 Federal Information Security Management Act

FISMA requires federal agencies to provide appropriate protection of their resources through implementing a comprehensive information security program that is commensurate with the sensitivity of the information being processed, transmitted, and stored by agency information systems. It also requires agencies to assess and report their performance in implementing and managing their information security programs.

The purpose of FISMA is to:

- Provide a comprehensive framework for ensuring the effectiveness of security controls over information resources that support federal operations and assets;
- Recognize the highly networked nature of the current federal computing environment and provide effective government wide management and oversight of related information

---

[4] Public Law 103-62, Government Performance and Results Act of 1993.

[5] OMB Circular A-11, *Preparation, Submission, and Execution of the Budget, 2005*, Section 15, clause 15.5.

security risks, including coordination of information security efforts throughout the civilian, national security, and law enforcement communities;

- Provide for the development and maintenance of minimum security controls required to protect federal information and information systems;
- Provide a mechanism for improved oversight of federal agency information security programs;
- Acknowledge that commercially developed information security products offer advanced, dynamic, robust, and effective information security solutions for the protection of critical information infrastructures important to national defense and economic security that are designed, built, and operated by the private sector; and
- Recognize that the selection of specific technical hardware and software information security solutions should be made by individual agencies from among commercially developed products.[6]

FISMA also mandated NIST to develop and promulgate standards and guidelines pertaining to federal information systems.

FISMA requires agencies to identify and assess risks to their information systems and define and implement appropriate security controls to protect their information resources. It also requires agencies to report quarterly and annually on the status of their information security programs. An institutionalized information security performance measurement program enables agencies to collect and report on relevant FISMA performance indicators. For example, information security performance measures enable agencies to quickly determine the percentage of their systems that are certified and accredited, the percentage of their personnel that have taken required information security training, and their compliance with other FISMA reporting requirements. A mature information security measurement program also enables agencies to satisfy any new information security performance measures reporting requirements required internally or externally by providing a basis for information security data collection, analysis, quantification, and reporting.

OMB publishes annual guidelines on the process and elements of annual and quarterly FISMA reporting.

4.2 Federal Enterprise Architecture

In addition to legislative information security performance measurement requirements, the Executive Branch periodically implements initiatives designed to monitor and improve the effectiveness of federal organizations. One such Executive Branch initiative that relies on information security measures is the Federal Enterprise Architecture (FEA). One of FEA's reference models is the Performance Reference Model (PRM). The PRM is a standardized

---

[6] Public Law 107-347, E-Government Act of 2002, Title III

framework to measure the performance of major IT investments and their contribution to program performance.

Organizations should consider tying information security measures development and implementation into FEA efforts to reduce duplication of data collection and facilitate integration of information security into their enterprise architectures.

4.3 Linkage Between Enterprise Strategic Planning and Information Security

Federal agencies develop their long-term strategic goals as part of their strategic planning process—a requirement of GPRA. Five to six strategic goals are usually established, each with several performance objectives that describe how the goal will be accomplished. As a part of this process, agencies develop performance measures to quantify the accomplishment of their goals and objectives with quarterly and annual targets for each performance measure.

Information security performance measures provide a means to monitor and report on an agency's implementation of its information security program and associated performance measures as mandated by FISMA. These measures can also help assess the effectiveness of security controls in protecting agency information resources in support of the agency's mission.

Ultimately, all efforts must support the agency's overall goals and objectives, which are defined and reassessed annually during its strategic planning activities. Information security must be explicitly tied to at least one goal or objective in the strategic planning process to demonstrate its importance in accomplishing the agency's mission. This connection can be established by identifying goals and objectives that would articulate agency information security requirements within the context of the overall agency mission. Progress toward accomplishing these goals and objectives may be monitored by implementing appropriate information security performance measures.

Information security performance measures can be developed and used at multiple levels within an organization—including the overall agency information security program, operating bureau information security programs, or individual agency programs. They can also be scoped to different types of efforts, as discussed in Section 3.6. Measures developed at different levels of an organization should be used for internal management and process improvement purposes. They may also be aggregated to agency-level information security program performance measures. Agency-level measures will either be reported to the organization's upper management or used for external reporting—such as GPRA and FISMA.

5. MEASURES DEVELOPMENT PROCESS

The benefit of devoting the time to set up an information security performance measures program in advance is similar to that of allowing time for requirements definition during information system development—investing time early in the process is more effective than retrofitting requirements once the effort is under way. Important considerations for setting up an information security performance measures program include:

- Selecting the measures most appropriate for the organization's strategy and business environment, including mission and information security priorities, environment, and requirements;

- Taking time to collect input and get buy-in from, and provide education to, all relevant stakeholders; and

- Ensuring that appropriate technical and process infrastructure is in place, including creation/modification of data collection, analysis, and reporting tools.

Two processes—measures development and measures implementation—guide the establishment and operation of an information security measurement program. The measures development process establishes the initial set of measures as well as selection of the measures subset that is appropriate for an organization at a given time. The information security measurement program implementation process is iterative by nature and ensures that appropriate aspects of information security are measured for a specific time period. The remainder of this section describes the measures development process. (Section 6 describes the information security measurement program implementation process.)

Figure 5-1 illustrates the place of information security measures within a larger organizational context and demonstrates that they can be used to progressively measure the implementation, effectiveness/efficiency, and business impact of information security activities within organizations or for specific information systems.

The information security measures development process consists of two major activities:

- Identification and definition of the current information security program; and

- Development and selection of specific measures to gauge the implementation, effectiveness, efficiency, and impact of the security controls.

The activities outlined in Figure 5-1 need not be done sequentially. The process is provided as a way to think about measures and facilitate the identification of measures tailored to a specific organization and its different stakeholder groups.

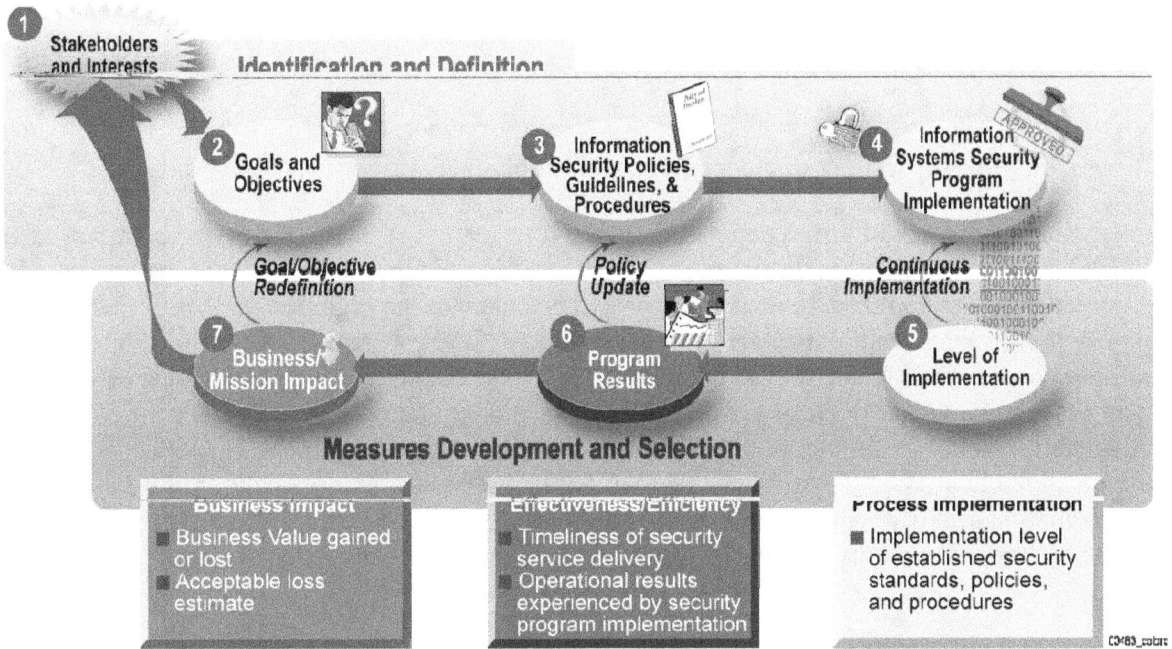

Figure 5-1. Information Security Measures Development Process

5.1 Stakeholder Interest Identification

Phase 1 of the measures development process (see Figure 5-1) identifies relevant stakeholders and their interests in information security measurement. Anyone within an organization can be an information security stakeholder, although some individuals or groups have a greater stake than others. The primary information security stakeholders are:

- Agency Head;
- CIO;
- SAISO/CISO;
- ISSO;
- Program manager/information system owner;
- Information system administrator/network administrator;
- Security engineers; and
- Information system support personnel.

Secondary information security stakeholders are members of groups within an organization that do not have information security as their primary mission but are involved with information security in some aspects of their operations. Examples of secondary information security stakeholders may include:

- Chief Financial Officer (CFO);

- Training organization;
- Human resources/personnel organization;
- Inspectors General (IG); and
- Chief Privacy Officer or other designated official with privacy responsibilities.

Stakeholder interests will differ, depending on the information security aspects of their particular role and their position within the organizational hierarchy. Each stakeholder may require an additional set of customized measures that provides a view of the organization's information security performance within their area of responsibility. Interests may be determined through multiple venues, such as interviews, brainstorming sessions, and mission statement reviews. In many cases, stakeholder interests are driven by laws and regulations. As referenced in Section 3.4.2, each stakeholder should initially be responsible for two to three measures. It is recommended that fewer measures per stakeholder be used when an organization is establishing an information security program; the number of measures per stakeholder should gradually increase as the information security program and information security measurement program mature.

Stakeholders should be involved in each step of information security measures development to ensure organizational buy-in to the concept of measuring information security performance. This involvement will also ensure that a sense of ownership of the information system security measures exists at multiple levels of the organization to encourage the program's overall success.

The three measurable aspects of information security—business impact, efficiency/effectiveness, and implementation—speak to different stakeholders. For example, an executive will be interested in the business and mission impact of information security activities (e.g., What is the monetary and public trust cost of the latest incident? Is there an article about us in a major newspaper?), information security and program managers will be interested in the effectiveness/efficiency of information security programs (e.g., Could we have prevented the incident? How fast did we respond to it?), and information systems or network administrators will want to know what went wrong (e.g., Have we performed all necessary steps to avoid or minimize the impact of the incident?).

5.2 Goals and Objectives Definition

Phase 2 of the measures development process (see Figure 5-1) is to identify and document information system security performance goals and objectives that would guide security control implementation for the information security program of a specific information system. For federal information systems, these goals and objectives may be expressed in the form of high-level policies and requirements, laws, regulations, guidelines, and guidance.[7]

---

[7] See Section 4 for additional information on requirements, laws, regulations, guidelines, and guidance.

Information security program goals and objectives can also be derived from enterprise-level goals and objectives in support of the overall organization's mission, which are usually articulated in agency strategic and performance plans. Applicable documents should be reviewed to identify and extract applicable information security performance goals and objectives. Extracted goals and objectives should be validated with the organizational stakeholders to ensure their acceptance of, and participation in, the measures development process.

Federal Information Processing Standard (FIPS) 200, *Minimum Security Requirements for Federal Information and Information Systems,* provides specifications for minimum security requirements. NIST SP 800-53 provides minimum security controls corresponding to low-impact, moderate-impact, and high-impact categories as defined in FIPS 199, *Standards for Security Categorization of Federal Information and Information Systems.* Agencies must define and implement minimum security controls based on the sensitivity of data processed, stored, and transmitted on their information systems. As such, agency information security programs must include planning, implementing, monitoring, and reporting on the implementation and effectiveness of these information system security controls. To facilitate explicit linkage of information security activities with agency-level strategic planning, agencies can use specifications for minimum security requirements, stated in FIPS 200, as an input into objectives for developing information security performance measures. (These specifications, which correspond to the 17 security control families in NIST SP 800-53, are provided in Appendix D. Appendix A provides candidate information security measures from both programmatic and system-level perspectives, with corresponding goals and objectives.)

5.3 Information Security Policies, Guidelines, and Procedures Review

Phase 3 of the measures development process (see Figure 5-1) focuses on organization-specific information security practices. Details of how security controls should be implemented are usually set forth in organization-specific policies and procedures that define a baseline of information security practices for the information system. Specifically, they describe how implementing security controls, requirements, and techniques lead to accomplishing information security performance goals and objectives. These documents should be examined not only during initial measures development, but in future measures development activities when the initial list of measures is exhausted and needs to be replaced. Applicable documents should be reviewed to identify information security controls, applicable processes, and targets of performance.

5.4 Information Security Program Implementation Review

In Phase 4 of the measures development process (see Figure 5-1), any existing measures and data repositories that can be used to derive measures data should be reviewed. Following the review, applicable information should be extracted and used to identify appropriate implementation evidence to support measures development and data collection.[8] Implementation evidence points to aspects of security controls that would be indicative of the information security performance objective being met, or at least that actions leading to the accomplishment of the performance objective in the future are performed. The information system security requirements, processes, and procedures that have been implemented can be extracted by consulting multiple sources, including documents, interviews, and observation.

The following sources may contain information from which measures data can be generated:

- System Security Plans;[9]
- Plan of Action and Milestones (POA&M) reports;
- Latest GAO and IG findings;
- Tracking of information security-related activities, such as incident handling and reporting, testing, network management, audit logs, and network and information system billing;
- Risk assessments and penetration testing results;
- C&A documentation (e.g., security assessment reports);
- Continuous monitoring results;
- Contingency plans;
- Configuration management plans; and
- Training results and statistics.

As information system security practices evolve and the documents that describe them change, existing measures will be retired and new measures will be developed. To ensure that the newly developed measures are appropriate, these and similar documents will need to be examined to identify new areas that should be captured in measures.

5.5 Measures Development and Selection

Phases 5, 6, and 7 of the measures development process, depicted in Figure 5-1, involve developing measures that track process implementation, efficiency/effectiveness, and mission impact. The performance measures development process presented in this section describes how to develop measures in these three areas for information security. (Appendix A provides candidate measures, some of which correspond to selected security control families in NIST SP 800-53.) To support continuous improvement of security for information systems and programs, the process explicitly connects information security activities to the organization's strategic goals

---

[8] Implementation evidence refers to the data collected to support an information security performance measure. Implementation evidence is discussed in greater detail in Table 2 contained in Section 5.6.

[9] NIST SP 800-18 provides guidelines on System Security Plan development.

through development and use of performance measures. This approach assumes that organizations have multiple strategic goals, and that a single goal may require inputs from multiple measures.

5.5.1 Measures Development Approach

Depending on the scope of the measurement effort, development of information security measures should focus on gauging the security performance of a specific security control, a group of security controls, or a security program. Such an approach will result in measures that help determine where a given organization stands in support of the corresponding strategic objective—and, when multiple controls or the entire program are being measured, provide a broad view of information security performance.

Measures corresponding to security control families or individual security controls should:

- Be mapped directly to the individual security control(s);
- Use data describing the security control's implementation to generate required measures such as POA&M, testing, and project tracking; and
- Characterize the measure as applicable to low, moderate, or high information system categorization.

Measures dealing with overall information security program performance should:

- Be mapped to information security goals and objectives that may encompass performance of information security across the spectrum of security controls; and
- Use the data describing the information security program performance to generate required measures.

5.5.2 Measures Prioritization and Selection

The universe of possible measures, based on existing policies and procedures, will be quite large. Measures must be prioritized to ensure that the set selected for initial implementation has the following qualities:

- Facilitates improvement of high-priority security control implementation as defined using a risk-based approach. "High priority" may be defined by the latest GAO or IG reports, results of a risk assessment, through continuous monitoring, or based on an internal organizational goal.
- Uses data that can realistically be obtained from existing sources and data repositories (e.g., system inventories, training databases, POA&Ms).

> Organizations manage what they measure. It is important to select two to three high-priority measures per stakeholder, determined by using a risk-based approach.

- Measures processes that already exist and are established. Measuring inconsistent processes will not provide meaningful data about information security performance and will not be useful for targeting specific aspects of performance. However, attempting such measurement may still be useful to attain a baseline to be closely monitored through continuous assessment and further measurement to improve the information security posture.

Organizations may decide to use a weighting scale to differentiate the importance of selected measures and ensure that results accurately reflect existing information security program priorities. This would involve assigning values to each measure based on its importance in the context of the overall information security program. Weight should be based on the overall risk mitigation goals and would likely reflect higher criticality of enterprise-level initiatives versus smaller-scale initiatives. This scale is a useful tool that facilitates the integration of information security measures into the departmental capital planning process.

5.5.3 Establishing Performance Targets

Establishing performance targets is an important component of defining information security measures. Performance targets establish a benchmark by which success is measured. The degree of success is based on the proximity of the measure result to the stated performance target. The mechanics of establishing performance targets differ for implementation measures and the other two types of measures (effectiveness/efficiency and impact). For implementation measures, targets are set to 100 percent completion of specific tasks.

Setting performance targets for effectiveness/efficiency and impact measures is complex because management will need to apply qualitative and subjective reasoning to determine appropriate levels of security effectiveness and efficiency, and use these levels as targets of performance for applicable measures. Although every organization desires effective implementation of security controls, efficient delivery of security services, and minimal impact of security events on its mission, the associated measurements will be different for different systems. An organization can attempt to establish performance targets for these measures and should be ready to adjust these targets, based on actual measurements, once they are obtained. The organization may also decide not to set targets for these measures until the first measurement is collected that can be used as a performance baseline. Once the baseline is obtained and corrective actions identified, appropriate measurement targets and implementation milestones that are realistic for a specific system environment can be defined. If performance targets cannot be established after the baseline has been obtained, management should evaluate whether the measured activities and corresponding measures are providing the expected value for the organization.

Establishment of effectiveness/efficiency and impact measures baselines and targets of performance can be facilitated if historic data that pertains to these measures is available. Trends observed in the past will provide insight into ranges of performance that have existed previously, and guide the creation of realistic targets for the future. In the future, expert recommendations and standards within the industry, when published, may provide a means of setting targets. Figure 5-2 provides an example of an implementation measure that is based on the percentage of approved system security plans.

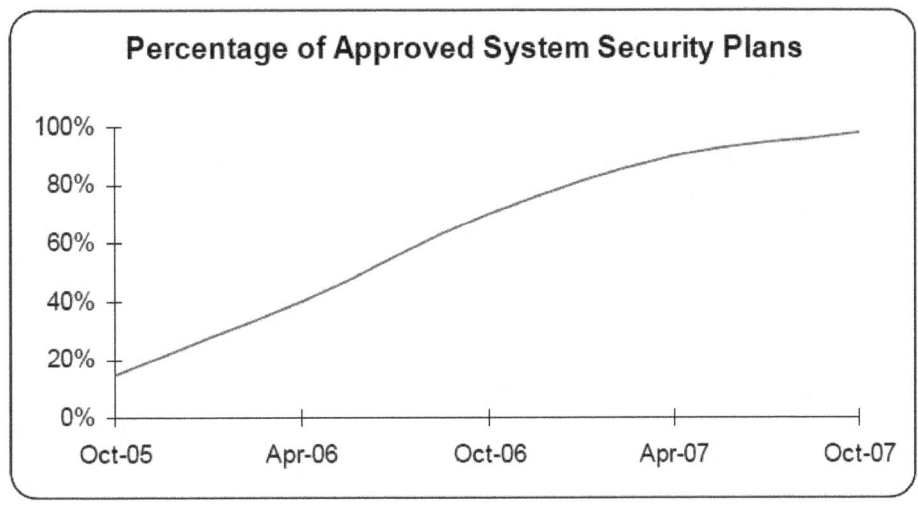

Figure 5-2. Information Security Measures Trend Example

5.6 Measures Development Template

Organizations should document their performance measures in a standard format to ensure repeatability of measures development, tailoring, collection, and reporting activities. A standard format will provide the detail required to guide measures collection, analysis, and reporting activities. The measures template, provided in Table 2, is an example of such a format.

While the measures template provides a suggested approach for measurement, depending upon internal practices and procedures, organizations may tailor their own performance measurement templates by using a subset of the provided fields or adding more fields based on their environment and requirements.

> This template and the candidate measures provided in Appendix A are examples, and are meant to be tailored to fit the needs of the organization.

Table 2. Measures Template and Instructions

Field	Data
Measure ID	State the unique identifier used for measure tracking and sorting. The unique identifier can be from an organization-specific naming convention or can directly reference another source.
Goal	Statement of strategic goal and/or information security goal. For system-level security control measures, the goal would guide security control implementation for that information system. For program-level measures, both strategic goals and information security goals can be included. For example, information security goals can be derived from enterprise-level goals in support of the organization's mission. These goals are usually articulated in strategic and performance plans. When possible, include both the enterprise-level goal and the specific information security goal extracted from agency documentation, or identify an information security program goal that would contribute to the accomplishment of the selected strategic goal.
Measure	Statement of measurement. Use a numeric statement that begins with the word "percentage," "number," "frequency," "average," or a similar term. If applicable, list the NIST SP 800-53 security control(s) being measured. Security controls that provide supporting data should be stated in Implementation Evidence. If the measure is applicable to a specific FIPS 199 impact level (high, moderate, or low), state this level within the measure.
Type	Statement of whether the measure is implementation, effectiveness/efficiency, or impact.
Formula	Calculation to be performed that results in a numeric expression of a measure. The information gathered through listing implementation evidence serves as an input into the formula for calculating the measure.
Target	Threshold for a satisfactory rating for the measure, such as milestone completion or a statistical measure. Target can be expressed in percentages, time, dollars, or other appropriate units of measure. Target may be tied to a required completion time frame. Select final and interim target to enable tracking of progress toward stated goal.
Implementation Evidence	Implementation evidence is used to compute the measure, validate that the activity is performed, and identify probable causes of unsatisfactory results for a specific measure. • For manual data collection, identify questions and data elements that would provide the data inputs necessary to calculate the measure's formula, qualify the measure for acceptance, and validate provided information. • For each question or query, state the security control number from NIST SP 800-53 that provides information, if applicable. • If the measure is applicable to a specific FIPS 199 impact level, questions should state the impact level. • For automated data collection, identify data elements that would be required for the formula, qualify the measure for acceptance, and validate the information provided.
Frequency	Indication of how often the data is collected and analyzed, and how often the data is reported. Select the frequency of data collection based on a rate of change in a particular security control that is being evaluated. Select the frequency of data reporting based on external reporting requirements and internal customer preferences.

Field	Data
Responsible Parties	Indicate the following key stakeholders: - Information Owner: Identify organizational component and individual who owns required pieces of information; - Information Collector: Identify the organizational component and individual responsible for collecting the data. (Note: If possible, Information Collector should be a different individual or even a representative of a different organizational unit than the Information Owner, to avoid the possibility of conflict of interest and ensure separation of duties. Smaller organizations will need to determine whether it is feasible to separate these two responsibilities.); and - Information Customer: Identify the organizational component and individual who will receive the data.
Data Source	Location of the data to be used in calculating the measure. Include databases, tracking tools, organizations, or specific roles within organizations that can provide required information.
Reporting Format	Indication of how the measure will be reported, such as a pie chart, line chart, bar graph, or other format. State the type of format or provide a sample.

Candidate measures provided in Appendix A are examples of information security measures and may or may not be required for regulatory or organizational reporting at any point in time (e.g., FISMA). The purpose of listing these measures is to demonstrate examples of measures that can be:

- Used as stated;
- Modified and tailored to a specific organization's requirement; or
- Used as a template for other information security measures.

Organizations are encouraged, but not required, to use these measures as a starting point for their information security measurement efforts.

5.7 Feedback Within the Measures Development Process

Measures that are ultimately selected for implementation will be useful not only for measuring performance, identifying causes of unsatisfactory performance, and pinpointing improvement areas, but also for facilitating consistent policy implementation, effecting information security policy changes, redefining goals and objectives, and supporting continuous improvement. This relationship is depicted by the feedback arrows in Figure 5-1, which are marked as Goal/Objective Redefinition, Policy Update, and Continuous Improvement. Once measurement of security control implementation begins, subsequent measures can be used to identify performance trends and determine whether the implementation rate is appropriate. A specific frequency of each measure collection will depend on the life cycle of a measured event. For example, a measure that pertains to the percentage of completed or updated system security plans should not be collected more often than semiannually, while a measure that pertains to crackable passwords should be collected more frequently. Over time, measurements will point to continuous implementation of applicable security controls. Once effectiveness/efficiency measures are implemented, they will facilitate an understanding of whether the security control performance goals, identified in the information security policies and procedures, are realistic and appropriate.

For example, if an information security policy defines a specific password configuration, compliance with this policy could be determined by measuring the percentage of passwords that are configured according to the policy. This measure addresses the level of security control implementation. It is assumed that configuring all passwords according to the policy will significantly reduce, if not eliminate, information system compromises through broken passwords. To measure effectiveness of the existing password policy implementation, the percentage of passwords crackable by common password-breaking tools could be identified. This measure addresses the effectiveness of the security control as implemented. If a significant percentage of crackable passwords remains after the required password policy has been implemented, the logical conclusion is that the underlying policy may be ineffective in thwarting password compromises. If this is the case, an organization will need to consider strengthening the policy or implementing other mitigating measures. Costs and benefits of keeping the password policy as is, tightening it, or replacing password authentication with other techniques must also be determined. Conducting cost-benefit analyses will generate business impact measures to address the issue of redefining information system identification and authentication objectives and appropriately realign these objectives with the information system mission.

6. INFORMATION SECURITY MEASUREMENT IMPLEMENTATION

Information security measurement implementation involves applying measures for monitoring information security control performance and using the results to initiate performance improvement actions. The information security measurement program implementation process consists of six phases, which, when fully executed, will ensure continuous use of these measures for security control performance monitoring and improvement. The process is shown in Figure 6-1.

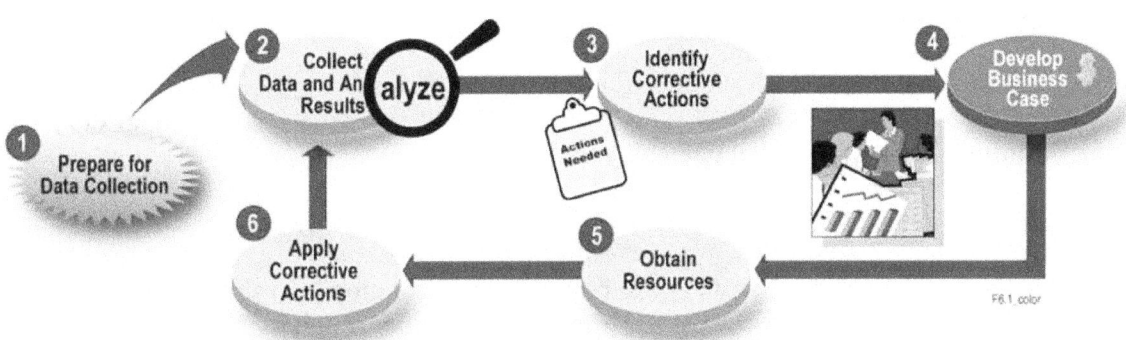

Figure 6-1. Information Security Measurement Program Implementation Process

6.1 Prepare for Data Collection

Phase 1 of the information security measurement program implementation process, *Prepare for Data Collection*, involves activities that are essential for establishing a comprehensive information security measurement program—including information security measures identification, definition, development, and selection. The next step is to develop an information security measurement program implementation plan.[10]

Specific implementation steps should be defined based on how data for the measures should be collected, analyzed, and reported. These steps should be documented in the measurement program implementation plan. The following items may be included in the plan:

---

[10] The information security measurement program implementation plan can be formal or informal, depending upon the organization's needs.

- Audience for the plan;

- Measurement roles and responsibilities, including responsibilities for data collection (both soliciting and submitting), analysis, and reporting;

- Process of measures collection, analysis, and reporting, as tailored to the specific organizational structure, processes, policies, and procedures;

- Details of coordination within the Office of the CIO, relating to areas such as risk assessment, C&A, and FISMA reporting activities;

- Details of coordination between the SAISO and other functions within the agency (e.g., physical security, personnel security, and privacy) to ensure that measures data collection is streamlined and non-intrusive;

- Creation or selection of data collection and tracking tools;

- Modifications of data collection and tracking tools; and

- Measures summary reporting formats.

Additionally, the information security measurement implementation plan should contain provisions for continuous monitoring of the information security program. Continuous monitoring activities include configuration management, information security impact analyses of changes to the information system, assessment of a subset of security controls, and status reporting. Sound continuous monitoring practices dictate that the organization establishes selection criteria for a subset of the security controls employed within the information system for purposes of continuous monitoring. NIST SP 800-37 provides guidelines on the continuous monitoring process. NIST SP 800-53A provides guidelines on the assessment of security controls. Results generated from continuous monitoring provide data necessary to support and supplement the data collected in Phase 2, and help facilitate corrective action prioritization in Phase 3.

6.2 Collect Data and Analyze Results

Phase 2 of the information security measurement program implementation process, *Collect Data and Analyze Results*, involves activities essential for ensuring that the collected measures are used to gain an understanding of information system security and identify appropriate improvement actions. This phase includes the following activities:

- Collect measures data according to the processes defined in the Measurement Program Implementation Plan;

- Aggregate measures as appropriate to derive higher-level measures (e.g., "rolling up" information system-level measures to derive program-level measures);

- Consolidate collected data and store in a format conducive to data analysis and reporting—for example, in a database or spreadsheet;

- Conduct gap analysis to compare collected measurements with targets (if defined) and identify gaps between actual and desired performance;

- Identify causes of poor performance; and

- Identify areas that require improvement.

Causes of poor performance can often be identified by using the data from more than one measure. For example, determining that the percentage of approved system security plans is unacceptably low would not be helpful for determining how to correct the problem. To determine the cause of low compliance, information will need to be obtained regarding the reasons for the low percentages (e.g., lack of guidelines, insufficient expertise, or conflicting priorities). This can be collected as separate measures or as implementation evidence for the percentage of approved system security plans. Once this information is collected and compiled, corrective actions could be directed at the cause of the problem.

The following are examples of factors contributing to poor security implementation and effectiveness:

- Resources—Insufficient human, monetary, or other resources;

- Training—Lack of appropriate training for personnel installing, administering, maintaining, or using the information systems;

- Information system upgrades—Information security patches that have been removed but not replaced during information system upgrades;

- Configuration management practices—New or upgraded information systems that are not configured with required information security settings and patches;

- Software compatibility—Information security patches or upgrades that are incompatible with software applications supported by the information system;

- Awareness and commitment—Lack of management awareness and/or commitment to information security;

- Policies and procedures—Lack of policies and procedures required to ensure existence, use, and audit of required information security functions;

- Architectures—Poor information system and information security architectures that render information systems vulnerable; and

- Inefficient processes—Inefficient planning and implementation processes that influence measures, including the communication processes necessary to direct organizational actions.

6.3 Identify Corrective Actions

Phase 3 of the information security measurement program implementation process, *Identify Corrective Actions*, involves development of a plan to serve as the roadmap for closing the implementation gap identified in Phase 2. It includes the following activities:

- Determine range of corrective actions—Based on results and causation factors, identify potential corrective actions for each performance issue. These may include changing information system configurations; training information security staff, information system administrator staff, or regular users; purchasing information security tools; changing information system architecture; establishing new processes and procedures; and updating information security policies.

- Prioritize corrective actions based on overall risk mitigation goals—Several corrective actions may apply to a single performance issue; however, some may be inappropriate if they are too costly or are inconsistent with the magnitude of the problem. Applicable corrective actions should be prioritized for each performance issue in ascending order of cost and descending order of impact. The risk management process described in NIST SP 800-30, *Risk Management Guide for Information Technology Systems*, or the corrective action prioritization process described in NIST SP 800-65, *Integrating IT Security into the Capital Planning and Investment Control Process,* should be used to prioritize corrective actions. If weights were assigned to measures in the *Prepare for Data Collection* phase, they should be used to prioritize corrective actions. Alternatively, priorities may be assigned in the *Identify Corrective Actions* phase based on the criticality of implementing specific corrective actions, cost of the actions, and the magnitude of their impact on the organization's information security posture. Corrective actions should be documented in the POA&M for the corresponding information system or organization and tracked as a part of the continuous monitoring process.

- Select most appropriate corrective actions—Viable corrective actions from the top of the prioritized list should be selected for use in a full cost-benefit analysis.

6.4 Develop Business Case and Obtain Resources

Phase 4 of the information security measurement program implementation process, *Develop Business Case*, and Phase 5, *Obtain Resources*, address the budgeting cycle for acquiring resources needed to implement remediation actions identified in Phase 3. The steps involved in developing a business case are based on industry practices and mandatory guidelines, including OMB Circular A-11, the Clinger-Cohen Act, and GPRA. Results of the prior three phases will be included in the business case as supporting evidence.

The following activities are generally performed as a part of business case analysis. They are pursued within the bounds of agency-specific processes to obtain the resources needed to implement corrective actions, and include:

- Document mission and objectives (identified during Phase 2 of the measures development process);

- Determine the cost and risks of maintaining status quo to use as a baseline for comparing investment alternatives;

- Document the information security performance gaps between target performance and current performance, as evidenced by the current measures collected during Phase 2 of the information security measurement program implementation process;

- Estimate the life cycle costs of each corrective action or investment alternative, as identified in Phase 3 of the information security measurement program implementation process;

- Perform sensitivity analysis to determine which variables have the greatest effect on the cost;[11]

- Characterize benefits that are quantifiable and non-quantifiable returns delivered through improved performance, based on the prioritization of corrective actions performed in Phase 3 of the information security measurement program implementation process;

- Perform risk analysis to assess the likelihood of obstacles and programmatic risks inherent to a particular alternative; and

- Prepare budget submission by summarizing key aspects of the business case to accurately illustrate its merits.[12]

Each agency should follow its specific business case guidelines during this phase of the process. Agencies typically have unique business case processes and life cycle spending thresholds that determine which investments and budget requests require a formal business case. In general, the level of effort to develop the business case should correspond with the size and scope of the funding request. For example, the business case to build and maintain a disaster recovery site would be more thorough than a business case to establish an account review process.

Regardless of the scope and complexity of the business case, its underlying components and analysis enable easier completion of internal and external budget requests. A thorough

---

[11] If a small change in the value of a variable causes a large change in the calculation result, the result is said to be sensitive to that parameter or assumption.

[12] See *NIST SP 800-65, Integrating IT Security Into the Capital Planning and Investment Control Process*, for more information on how to prepare appropriate budget request information for corrective actions.

examination of the business case will support and facilitate the *Obtain Resources* phase, which involves the following activities:

- Respond to budget evaluation inquiries;
- Receive allocated budget;
- Prioritize available resources (if all requested resources are not allocated); and
- Assign resources to perform corrective actions.

6.5 Apply Corrective Actions

Phase 6 of the information security measurement program implementation process, *Apply Corrective Actions*, involves implementing corrective actions in the security program, or in the technical, management, and operational areas of security controls. The POA&M process is used to document and monitor the corrective action status.

Iterative data collection, analysis, and reporting will track the progress of corrective actions, measure improvement, and identify areas where further improvement is needed. The nature of the cycle monitors progress and ensures that corrective actions are influencing information system security control implementation in the intended way. Frequent performance measurements will flag actions that are not implemented as planned or do not have the desired effect, enabling quick course corrections within the organization to avoid problems that could be uncovered during external audits, C&A efforts, or related activities.

Appendix A: CANDIDATE MEASURES

> *Devoting sufficient time to establishing information security performance measures is critical to deriving the maximum value from measuring information security performance.*

This section offers a sampling of program-level and system-level measures. The sample measures include information security programmatic measures, and measures that align with the minimum security requirements in Federal Information Processing Standard (FIPS) 200, *Minimum Security Requirements for Federal Information and Information Systems*, which correspond to the 17 security control families in NIST SP 800-53. They are not intended for adoption as a complete set, but are provided as examples that organizations can tailor and adapt to measure the performance of their information security programs. Examples of tailoring include specific time frames, implementation evidence, data sources, formulas, reporting formats, frequency, responsible parties, or adding further fields to the template.

It should be noted that these measures do not completely address the minimum security requirements from FIPS 200, but will address one or more important aspects of the requirements. Organizations should look into developing additional measures to complement or replace those provided in this section if the samples are not appropriate for their needs.

These candidate measures offer examples of specific security controls implemented at the program level or at the system level and include all measure types—implementation, effectiveness/efficiency, and impact.

Measure 1: Security Budget (program-level)

Field	Data
Measure ID	Security Budget Measure 1
Goal	- *Strategic Goal:* Ensure an environment of comprehensive security and accountability for personnel, facilities, and products. - *Information Security Goal:* Provide resources necessary to properly secure agency information and information systems.
Measure	Percentage (%) of the agency's information system budget devoted to information security NIST SP 800-53 Controls – SA-2; Allocation of Resources
Measure Type	Impact
Formula	(Information security budget/total agency information technology budget) *100
Target	This should be an organizationally defined percentage.
Implementation Evidence	1. What is the total information security budget across all agency systems (SA-2)? _____ 2. What is the total information technology budget across all agency systems (SA-2)? _____
Frequency	Collection Frequency: Organization-defined (example: annually) Reporting Frequency: Organization-defined (example: annually)
Responsible Parties	- Information Owner: Chief Information Officer (CIO), Chief Financial Officer (CFO), Senior Agency Information Security Officer (SAISO) (e.g., Chief Information Security Officer [CISO]) - Information Collector: System Administrator or Information System Security Officer (ISSO), budget personnel - Information Customer: Chief Information Officer (CIO), Senior Agency Information Security Officer (SAISO) (e.g., Chief Information Security Officer [CISO]), external audiences (e.g., Office of Management and Budget)
Data Source	Exhibit 300s, Exhibit 53s, agency budget documentation
Reporting Format	Pie chart illustrating the total agency information technology budget and the portion of that budget devoted to information security

Measure 2: Vulnerability Management (program-level)

Field	Data
Measure ID	Vulnerability Measure 1
Goal	- *Strategic Goal:* Ensure an environment of comprehensive security and accountability for personnel, facilities, and products. - *Information Security Goal:* Ensure all vulnerabilities are identified and mitigated.
Measure	Percentage (%) of high[13] vulnerabilities mitigated within organizationally defined time periods after discovery NIST SP 800-53 Controls: RA-5; Vulnerability Scanning
Measure Type	Effectiveness/**Efficiency**
Formula	(Number of high vulnerabilities identified and mitigated within targeted time frame during the time period /number of high vulnerabilities identified within the time period) *100
Target	This should be a high percentage defined by the organization.
Implementation Evidence	1. Number of high vulnerabilities identified across the enterprise during the time period (RA-5)? _____ 2. Number of high vulnerabilities mitigated across the enterprise during the time period (RA-5)? _____
Frequency	Collection Frequency: Organization-defined (example: quarterly) Reporting Frequency: Organization-defined (example: quarterly)
Responsible Parties	- Information Owner: Chief Information Officer (CIO), Senior Agency Information Security Officer (SAISO) (e.g., Chief Information Security Officer [CISO]), System Owner - Information Collector: System Administrator or Information System Security Officer (ISSO) - Information Customer: Chief Information Officer (CIO), Senior Agency Information Security Officer (SAISO) (e.g., Chief Information Security Officer [CISO])
Data Source	Vulnerability scanning software, audit logs, vulnerability management systems, patch management systems, change management records
Reporting Format	Stacked bar chart illustrating the percentage of high vulnerabilities closed within targeted time frames after discovery over several reporting periods

---

[13] The National Vulnerability Database (NVD) provides severity rankings of "Low" "Medium" and "High" for all Common Vulnerabilities and Exposures (CVE) in the database. The NVD is accessible at http://nvd.nist.gov.

Measure 3: Access Control (AC) (system-level)

Field	Data
Measure ID	Remote Access Control Measure 1 (or a unique identifier to be filled out by the organization)
Goal	- *Strategic Goal:* Ensure an environment of comprehensive security and accountability for personnel, facilities, and products. - *Information Security Goal:* Restrict information, system, and component access to individuals or machines that are identifiable, known, credible, and authorized.
Measure	Percentage (%) of remote access points used to gain unauthorized access NIST SP 800-53 Controls: AC-17; Remote Access
Measure Type	**Effectiveness**/Efficiency
Formula	(Number of remote access points used to gain unauthorized access/total number of remote access points) *100
Target	This should be a low percentage defined by the organization.
Implementation Evidence	1. Does the organization use automated tools to maintain an up-to-date network diagram that identifies all remote access points (CM-2)? ☐ Yes ☐ No 2. How many remote access points exist in the organization's network? _____ 3. Does the organization employ Intrusion Detection Systems (IDS) to monitor traffic traversing remote access points (SI-4)? ☐ Yes ☐ No 4. Does the organization collect and review audit logs associated with all remote access points (AU-6)? ☐ Yes ☐ No 5. Does the organization maintain a security incident database that identifies standardized incident categories for each incident (IR-5)? ☐ Yes ☐ No 6. Based on reviews of the incident database, IDS logs and alerts, and/or appropriate remote access point log files, how many access points have been used to gain unauthorized access within the reporting period? _____
Frequency	Collection Frequency: Organization-defined (example: monthly) Reporting Frequency: Organization-defined (example: quarterly)
Responsible Parties	- Information Owner: Computer Security Incident Response Team (CSIRT) - Information Collector: System Administrator or Information System Security Officer (ISSO) - Information Customer: Chief Information Officer (CIO), Senior Agency Information Security Officer (SAISO) (e.g., Chief Information Security Officer [CISO])
Data Source	Incident database, audit logs, network diagrams, IDS logs and alerts
Reporting Format	Stacked bar chart, by month, which illustrates the percentage of remote access points used for unauthorized access versus the total number of remote access points

Measure 4: Awareness and Training (AT) (program-level)

Field	Data
Measure ID	Security Training Measure 1 (or a unique identifier to be filled out by the organization)
Goal	- *Strategic Goal:* Ensure a high-quality work force supported by modern and secure infrastructure and operational capabilities. - *Information Security Goal:* Ensure that organization personnel are adequately trained to carry out their assigned information security-related duties and responsibilities.
Measure	Percentage (%) of information system security personnel that have received security training NIST SP 800-53 Controls: AT-3: Security Training
Measure Type	Implementation
Formula	(Number of information system security personnel that have completed security training within the past year/total number of information system security personnel) *100
Target	This should be a high percentage defined by the organization.
Implementation Evidence	1. Are significant security responsibilities defined with qualifications criteria and documented in policy (AT-1 and PS-2)? ☐ Yes ☐ No 2. Are records kept of which employees have significant security responsibilities (AT-3)? ☐ Yes ☐ No 3. How many employees in your agency (or agency component, as applicable) have significant security responsibilities (AT-3)? _____ 4. Are training records maintained (AT-4)? (Training records indicate the training that specific employees have received.) ☐ Yes ☐ No 5. How many of those with significant security responsibilities have received the required training (AT-4)? _____ 6. If all personnel have not received training, state all reasons that apply (AT-4): ☐ Insufficient funding ☐ Insufficient time ☐ Courses unavailable ☐ Employee has not registered ☐ Other (specify) _____
Frequency	Collection Frequency: Organization-defined (example: quarterly) Reporting Frequency: Organization-defined (example: annually)
Responsible	- Information Owner: Organization-defined (example: Training Manager)

Field	Data
Parties	- Information Collector: Organization-defined (example: Information System Security Officer [ISSO], Training Manager) - Information Customer: Chief Information Officer (CIO), Information System Security Officer (ISSO), Senior Agency Information Security Officer (SAISO) (e.g., Chief Information Security Officer [CISO])
Data Source	Training and awareness tracking records
Reporting Format	Pie chart illustrating the percentage of security personnel that have received training versus those who have not received training. If performance is below target, pie chart illustrating causes of performance falling short of targets

Measure 5: Audit and Accountability (AU) (system-level)

Field	Data
Measure ID	Audit Record Review Measure 1 (or a unique identifier to be filled out by the organization)
Goal	- *Strategic Goal:* Ensure an environment of comprehensive security and accountability for personnel, facilities, and products. - *Information Security Goal:* Create, protect, and retain information system audit records to the extent needed to enable the monitoring, analysis, investigation, and reporting of unlawful, unauthorized, or inappropriate activity.
Measure	Average frequency of audit records review and analysis for inappropriate activity NIST SP 800-53 Controls: AU-6: Audit Monitoring, Analysis, and Reporting
Measure Type	Effectiveness/**Efficiency**
Formula	Average frequency during reporting period
Target	This should be a high frequency defined by the organization.
Implementation Evidence	For each system: 1. Is logging activated on the system (AU-2)? ☐ Yes ☐ No 2. Does the organization have clearly defined criteria for what constitutes evidence of "inappropriate" activity within system audit logs? ☐ Yes ☐ No 3. For the reporting period, how many system audit logs have been reviewed within the following time frames for inappropriate activity (choose the nearest time period for each system) (AU-3 and AU-6): Within the past day _____ Within the past week _____ 2 weeks to 1 month _____ 1 month to 6 months _____ Over 6 months _____
Frequency	Collection Frequency: Organization-defined (example: daily) Reporting Frequency: Organization-defined (example: quarterly)
Responsible Parties	- Information Owner: Organization-defined (example: System Owner) - Information Collector: Organization-defined (example: System Administrator) - Information Customer: Chief Information Officer (CIO), Information System Security Officer (ISSO), Senior Agency Information Security Officer (SAISO) (e.g., Chief Information Security Officer [CISO])
Data Source	Audit log reports
Reporting Format	Bar chart showing the number of systems with average audit log reviews in each of the five categories within the Implementation Evidence field

Measure 6: Certification, Accreditation, and Security Assessments (CA) (program-level)

Field	Data
Measure ID	C&A Completion Measure 1 (or a unique identifier to be filled out by the organization)
Goal	- *Strategic Goal:* Ensure an environment of comprehensive security and accountability for personnel, facilities, and products. - *Information Security Goal:* Ensure all information systems have been certified and accredited as required.
Measure	Percentage (%) of new systems that have completed certification and accreditation (C&A) prior to their implementation NIST SP 800-53 Control: CA-6: Security Accreditation
Measure Type	**Effectiveness/Efficiency**
Formula	(Number of new systems with complete C&A packages with Authorizing Official [AO] approval prior to implementation)/(total number of new systems) *100
Target	This should be a high percentage defined by the organization.
Implementation Evidence	1. Does your agency (or agency component, if applicable) maintain a complete and up-to-date system inventory? ☐ Yes ☐ No 2. Is there a formal C&A process within your agency (CA-1)? ☐ Yes ☐ No 3. If the answer to Question 2 is yes, are system development projects required to complete C&A prior to implementation (CA-1)? ☐ Yes ☐ No 4. How many new systems have been implemented during the reporting period? _____ 5. How many systems indicated in Question 4 have received an authority to operate prior to implementation (CA-6)? _____
Frequency	Collection Frequency: Organization-defined (example: quarterly) Reporting Frequency: Organization-defined (example: annually)
Responsible Parties	- Information Owner: Organization-defined (example: Authorizing Official [AO]) - Information Collector: Organization-defined (example: System Owners) - Information Customer: Chief Information Officer (CIO), Information System Security Officer (ISSO), Senior Agency Information Security Officer (SAISO) (e.g., Chief Information Security Officer [CISO])
Data Source	System inventory, system C&A documentation
Reporting Format	Pie chart comparing the percentage of new systems with AO-approved C&A packages versus new systems without AO-approved C&A packages

Measure 7: Configuration Management (CM) (program-level)

Field	Data
Measure ID	Configuration Changes Measure 1 (or a unique identifier to be filled out by the organization)
Goal	- *Strategic Goal:* Accelerate the development and use of an electronic information infrastructure. - *Information Security Goal:* Establish and maintain baseline configurations and inventories of organizational information systems (including hardware, software, firmware, and documentation) throughout the respective system development life cycles.
Measure	Percentage (%) approved and implemented configuration changes identified in the latest automated baseline configuration NIST SP 800-53 Controls – CM-2: Baseline Configuration and CM-3: Configuration Change Control
Measure Type	Implementation
Formula	(Number of approved and implemented configuration changes identified in the latest automated baseline configuration/total number of configuration changes identified through automated scans) *100
Target	This should be a high percentage defined by the organization.
Implementation Evidence	1. Does the organization manage configuration changes to information systems using an organizationally approved process (CM-3)? ☐ Yes ☐ No 2. Does the organization use automated scanning to identify configuration changes that were implemented on its systems and networks (CM-2, Enhancement 2)? ☐ Yes ☐ No 3. If yes, how many configuration changes were identified through automated scanning over the last reporting period (CM-3)? _____ 4. How many change control requests were approved and implemented over the last reporting period (CM 3)? _____
Frequency	Collection Frequency: Organization-defined (example: quarterly) Reporting Frequency: Organization-defined (example: annually)
Responsible Parties	- Information Owner: Organization-defined (example: Configuration Manager) - Information Collector: Organization-defined (example: Information System Security Officer (ISSO), System Owner, System Administrator) - Information Customer: Chief Information Officer (CIO), Information System Security Officer (ISSO), Senior Agency Information Security Officer (SAISO) (e.g., Chief Information Security Officer [CISO]), Authorizing Official [AO], Configuration Control Board)
Data Source	System security plans, configuration management database, security tool logs
Reporting Format	Pie chart comparing the percentage of approved and implemented changes documented in the latest baseline configuration versus the percentage of changes not documented in the latest baseline configuration

Measure 8: Contingency Planning (CP) (program-level)

Field	Data
Measure ID	Contingency Plan Testing Measure 1 (or a unique identifier to be filled out by the organization)
Goal	- *Strategic Goal:* Ensure an environment of comprehensive security and accountability for personnel, facilities, and products. - *Information Security Goal:* Establish, maintain, and effectively implement plans for emergency response, backup operations, and post-disaster recovery for organizational information systems to ensure the availability of critical information resources and continuity of operations in emergency situations.
Measure	Percentage (%) of information systems that have conducted annual contingency plan testing NIST SP 800-53 Controls: CP-4: Contingency Plan Testing and Exercises
Measure Type	**Effectiveness/Efficiency**
Formula	(Number of information systems that have conducted annual contingency plans testing/number of information systems in the system inventory) *100
Target	This should be a high percentage defined by the organization.
Implementation Evidence	1. How many information systems are in the system inventory? _____ 2. How many information systems have an approved contingency plan (CP-2)? _____ 3. How many contingency plans were successfully tested within the past year (CP-4)? _____
Frequency	Collection Frequency: Organization-defined (example: annually) Reporting Frequency: Organization-defined (example: annually)
Responsible Parties	- Information Owner: Organization-defined (example: Contingency Plan Manager) - Information Collector: Organization-defined (example: System Owner, System Administrator) - Information Customer: Chief Information Officer (CIO), Information System Security Officer (ISSO), Senior Agency Information Security Officer (SAISO) (e.g., Chief Information Security Officer [CISO])
Data Source	Contingency Plan testing results
Reporting Format	Pie chart comparing the percentage of systems that conducted annual contingency plan testing versus the percentage of systems that have not conducted annual contingency plan testing

Measure 9: Identification and Authentication (IA) (system-level)

Field	Data
Measure ID	User Accounts Measure 1 (or a unique identifier to be filled out by the organization)
Goal	- *Strategic Goal:* Ensure an environment of comprehensive security and accountability for personnel, facilities, and products. - *Information Security Goal:* All system users are identified and authenticated in accordance with information security policy.
Measure	Percentage (%) of users with access to shared accounts NIST SP 800-53 Controls – AC-2: Account Management, AC-3: Access Enforcement, and IA-2: User Identification and Authentication
Measure Type	**Effectiveness/Efficiency**
Formula	(Number of users with access to shared accounts/total number of users) *100
Target	This should be a low percentage defined by the organization.
Implementation Evidence	1. How many users have access to the system (IA-2)? _____ 2. How many users have access to shared accounts (AC-2)? _____
Frequency	Collection Frequency: Organization-defined (example: monthly) Reporting Frequency: Organization-defined (example: monthly)
Responsible Parties	- Information Owner: Organization-defined (example: System Owner, System Administrator) - Information Collector: Organization-defined (example: System Administrator) - Information Customer: Chief Information Officer (CIO), Information System Security Officer (ISSO), Senior Agency Information Security Officer (SAISO) (e.g., Chief Information Security Officer [CISO])
Data Source	Configuration Management Database, Access Control List, System-Produced User ID Lists
Reporting Format	Pie chart comparing the percentage of users with access to shared accounts versus the percentage of users without access to shared accounts

Measure 10: Incident Response (IR) (program-level and system-level)

Field	Data
Measure ID	Incident Response Measure 1 (or a unique identifier to be filled out by the organization)
Goal	• *Strategic Goal:* Make accurate, timely information on the organization's programs and services readily available. • *Information Security Goal:* Track, document, and report incidents to appropriate organizational officials and/or authorities.
Measure	Percentage (%) of incidents reported within required time frame per applicable incident category (the measure will be computed for each incident category described in Implementation Evidence) NIST SP 800-53 Controls – IR-6: Incident Reporting
Measure Type	**Effectiveness**/Efficiency
Formula	For each incident category (number of incidents reported on time/total number of reported incidents) *100
Target	This should be a high percentage defined by the organization.
Implementation Evidence	1. How many incidents were reported during the period (IR-6)? Category 1 – Unauthorized Access? _____ Category 2 – Denial of Service? _____ Category 3 – Malicious Code? _____ Category 4 – Improper Usage? _____ Category 5 – Scans/Probes/Attempted Access? _____ Category 6 – Investigation? _____ 2. How many incidents involving personally identifiable information (PII) were reported during the period (IR-6)? _____ 3. Of the incidents reported, how many were reported within the prescribed time frame for their category, according to the time frames established by US-CERT (IR-6)? Category 1 – Unauthorized Access? _____ Category 2 – Denial of Service? _____ Category 3 – Malicious Code? _____ Category 4 – Improper Usage? _____ Category 5 – Scans/Probes/Attempted Access? _____ Category 6 – Investigation? _____ 4. Of the PII incidents reported, how many were reported within the prescribed time frame for their category, according to the time frames established by US-CERT and/or OMB Memorandum(s) (IR-6)? _____
Frequency	Collection Frequency: Organization-defined (example: monthly) Reporting Frequency: Organization-defined (example: annually)

Field	Data
Responsible Parties	• Information Owner: Organization-defined (example: Computer Security Incident Response Team [CSIRT]) • Information Collector: Organization-defined (example: System Owner, Information Security Officer [ISSO], CSIRT) • Information Customer: Chief Information Officer (CIO), Senior Agency Information Security Officer (SAISO) (e.g., Chief Information Security Officer [CISO])
Data Source	Incident logs, incident tracking database (if available)
Reporting Format	For one-time snapshot — stacked bar chart illustrating the proportion of reported incidents per category that were reported on time For trends — line chart where each line represents an individual category plus a line representing 100 percent

Measure 11: Maintenance (MA) (system-level)

Field	Data
Measure ID	Maintenance Measure 1 (or a unique identifier to be filled out by the organization)
Goal	- *Strategic Goal:* Accelerate the development and use of an electronic information infrastructure. - *Information Security Goal:* Perform periodic and timely maintenance on organizational information systems and provide effective controls on the tools, techniques, mechanisms, and personnel used to conduct information system maintenance.
Measure	Percentage (%) of system components that undergo maintenance in accordance with formal maintenance schedules NIST SP 800-53 Controls – MA-2: Controlled Maintenance and MA-6: Timely Maintenance
Measure Type	Effectiveness/**Efficiency**
Formula	(Number of system components that undergo maintenance according to formal maintenance schedules/total number of system components) *100
Target	This should be a high percentage defined by the organization.
Implementation Evidence	1. Does the system have a formal maintenance schedule (MA-2)? ☐ Yes ☐ No 2. How many components are contained within the system (CM-8)? _____ 3. How many components underwent maintenance in accordance with the formal maintenance schedule (MA-6)? _____
Frequency	Collection Frequency: Organization-defined (example: quarterly) Reporting Frequency: Organization-defined (example: annually)
Responsible Parties	- Information Owner: Organization-defined (example: System Owner) - Information Collector: Organization-defined (example: System Administrator) - Information Customer: Chief Information Officer (CIO), Information System Security Officer (ISSO), Senior Agency Information Security Officer (SAISO) (e.g., Chief Information Security Officer [CISO])
Data Source	Maintenance schedule, maintenance logs
Reporting Format	Pie chart comparing the percentage of system components receiving maintenance in accordance with the formal maintenance schedule versus the percentage of system components not receiving maintenance in accordance with the formal maintenance schedule over the specified period

Measure 12: Media Protection (MP) (program-level and system-level)

Field	Data
Measure ID	Media Sanitization Measure 1 (or a unique identifier to be filled out by the organization)
Goal	- *Strategic Goal:* Ensure an environment of comprehensive security and accountability for personnel, facilities, and products. - *Information Security Goal:* Sanitize or destroy information system media before disposal or release for reuse.
Measure	Percentage (%) of media that passes sanitization procedures testing for FIPS 199 high-impact systems NIST SP 800-53 Controls — MP-6: Media Sanitization and Disposal
Measure Type	**Effectiveness**/Efficiency
Formula	(Number of media that passes sanitization procedures testing/total number of media tested) * 100
Target	This should be a high percentage defined by the organization.
Implementation Evidence	1. Is there a policy for sanitizing media before it is discarded or reused (MP-1)? ☐ Yes ☐ No 2. Does the organization test media sanitization procedures for FIPS 199 high-impact systems (MP-6, Enhancement 2)? ☐ Yes ☐ No 3. Number of media that successfully passed sanitization testing for FIPS 199 high-impact systems (MP-6, Enhancement 2)? _____ 4. Total number of media tested for FIPS 199 high-impact systems (MP-6, Enhancement 2)? _____
Frequency	Collection Frequency: Organization-defined (example: quarterly) Reporting Frequency: Organization-defined (example: annually)
Responsible Parties	- Information Owner: Organization-defined (example: Facility Security Officer) - Information Collector: Organization-defined (example: System Owner, Information System Security Officer (ISSO]) - Information Customer: Chief Information Officer (CIO), Senior Agency Information Security Officer (SAISO) (e.g., Chief Information Security Officer [CISO])
Data Source	Sanitization testing results
Reporting Format	Pie chart comparing the percentage of media passing sanitization procedures testing versus the percentage of media not passing sanitization procedures testing over the specified period

Measure 13: Physical and Environmental (PE) (program-level)

Field	Data
Measure ID	Physical Security Incidents Measure 1 (or a unique identifier to be filled out by the organization)
Goal	- *Strategic Goal:* Ensure an environment of comprehensive security and accountability for personnel, facilities, and products. - *Information Security Goal:* Integrate physical and information security protection mechanisms to ensure appropriate protection of the organization's information resources.
Measure	Percentage (%) of physical security incidents allowing unauthorized entry into facilities containing information systems NIST SP 800-53 Control – PE-6: Monitoring Physical Access
Measure Type	**Effectiveness**/Efficiency
Formula	(Number of physical security incidents allowing unauthorized entry into facilities containing information systems/total number of physical security incidents) *100
Target	This should be a low percentage defined by the organization.
Implementation Evidence	1. How many physical security incidents occurred during the specified period (PE-6)? _____ 2. How many of the physical security incidents allowed unauthorized entry into facilities containing information systems (PE-6)? _____
Frequency	Collection Frequency: Organization-defined (example: quarterly) Reporting Frequency: Organization-defined (example: quarterly)
Responsible Parties	- Information Owner: Organization-defined (example: Physical Security Officer) - Information Collector: Organization-defined (example: Computer Security Incident Response Team [CSIRT]) - Information Customer: Chief Information Officer (CIO), Information System Security Officer (ISSO), Senior Agency Information Security Officer (SAISO) (e.g., Chief Information Security Officer [CISO])
Data Source	Physical security incident reports, physical access control logs
Reporting Format	Pie chart comparing the physical security incidents allowing unauthorized entry into facilities containing information systems versus the total number of physical security incidents

Measure 14: Planning (PL) (program-level and system-level)

Field	Data
Measure ID	Planning Measure 1 (or a unique identifier to be filled out by the organization)
Goal	- *Strategic Goal:* Ensure an environment of comprehensive security and accountability for personnel, facilities, and products.. - *Information Security Goal:* Develop, document, periodically update, and implement security plans for organizational information systems that describe the security controls in place or planned for information systems, and the rules of behavior for individuals accessing these systems.
Measure	Percentage of employees who are authorized access to information systems only after they sign an acknowledgement that they have read and understood rules of behavior NIST SP 800-53 Controls – PL-4: Rules of Behavior and AC-2: Account Management
Measure Type	Implementation
Formula	(Number of users who are granted system access after signing rules of behavior/total number of users with system access) *100
Target	This should be a high percentage defined by the organization.
Implementation Evidence	1. How many users access the system (AC-2)? _____ 2. How many users signed rules of behavior acknowledgements (PL-4)? _____ 3. How many users have been granted access to the information system only after signing rules of behavior acknowledgements? _____
Frequency	Collection Frequency: Organization-defined (example: quarterly) Reporting Frequency: Organization-defined (example: annually)
Responsible Parties	- Information Owner: Organization-defined (example: System Owner, Information System Security Officer [ISSO]) - Information Collector: Organization-defined (example: System Administrator, System Owner) - Information Customer: Chief Information Officer (CIO), Information System Security Officer (ISSO), Senior Agency Information Security Officer (SAISO) (e.g., Chief Information Security Officer [CISO])
Data Source	Repositories containing rules of behavior records
Reporting Format	Pie chart comparing the percentage of users who have signed rules of behavior acknowledgement forms prior to being granted information system access to those users who have accessed the system without signed rules of behavior acknowledgement forms

Measure 15: Personnel Security (PS) (program-level and system-level)

Field	Data
Measure ID	Personnel Security Screening Measure 1 (or a unique identifier to be filled out by the organization)
Goal	- *Strategic Goal:* Ensure an environment of comprehensive security and accountability for personnel, facilities, and products. - *Information Security Goal:* Ensure that individuals occupying positions of responsibility within organizations are trustworthy and meet established security criteria for those positions.
Measure	Percentage (%) of individuals screened before being granted access to organizational information and information systems NIST SP 800-53 Controls – AC-2: Account Management and PS-3: Personnel Screening
Measure Type	Implementation
Formula	(Number of individuals screened/total number of individuals with access) *100
Target	This should be a high percentage defined by the organization.
Implementation Evidence	1. How many individuals have been granted access to organizational information and information systems (AC-2)? _____ 2. What is the number of individuals who have completed personnel screening (PS-3)? _____
Frequency	Collection Frequency: Organization-defined (example: quarterly) Reporting Frequency: Organization-defined (example: annually)
Responsible Parties	- Information Owner: Organization-defined (example: Human Resources) - Information Collector: Organization-defined (example: System Administrators, System Owners, Information System Security Officer [ISSO]) - Information Customer: Chief Information Officer (CIO), Information System Security Officer (ISSO), Senior Agency Information Security Officer (SAISO) (e.g., Chief Information Security Officer [CISO])
Data Source	Clearance records, access control lists
Reporting Format	Pie chart comparing the percentage of individuals screened versus the total number of individuals

Measure 16: Risk Assessment (RA) (system-level)

Field	Data
Measure ID	Risk Assessment Vulnerability Measure 1 (or a unique identifier to be filled out by the organization)
Goal	• *Strategic Goal:* Ensure an environment of comprehensive security and accountability for personnel, facilities, and products. • *Information Security Goal:* Periodically assess the risk to organizational operations (including mission, functions, image, or reputation), organizational assets, and individuals resulting from the operation of organizational information systems.
Measure	Percentage (%) of vulnerabilities remediated within organization-specified time frames NIST SP 800-53 Controls – RA-5: Vulnerability Scanning and CA-5: Plan of Actions and Milestones
Measure Type	Effectiveness/**Efficiency**
Formula	(Number of vulnerabilities remediated according to POA&M schedule/total number of POA&M-documented vulnerabilities identified through vulnerability scans) *100
Target	This should be a high percentage defined by the organization.
Implementation Evidence	1. Does the organization conduct periodic vulnerability scans (RA-5)? ☐ Yes ☐ No 2. What is the periodicity of vulnerability scans (RA-5)? ☐ Weekly ☐ Monthly ☐ Quarterly ☐ Other _____ 3. Does the organization's POA&M process require vulnerabilities identified through vulnerability scanning to be documented in appropriate system POA&Ms (CA-5)? ☐ Yes ☐ No 4. How many vulnerabilities were identified through vulnerability scanning and entered into applicable POA&Ms (CA-5)? _____ 5. How many of the vulnerabilities from Question 4 were remediated on schedule according to their POA&Ms (CA-5)? _____
Frequency	Collection Frequency: Organization-defined (example: monthly) Reporting Frequency: Organization-defined (example: monthly)

Field	Data
Responsible Parties	- Information Owner: Organization-defined (example: System Owners, Information System Security Officer [ISSO]) - Information Collector: Organization-defined (example: System Administrators, System Owners, Information System Security Officer [ISSO]) - Information Customer: Chief Information Officer (CIO), Information System Security Officer (ISSO), Senior Agency Information Security Officer (SAISO) (e.g., Chief Information Security Officer [CISO])
Data Source	POA&Ms, vulnerability scanning reports
Reporting Format	Pie chart comparing the percentage of vulnerabilities remediated on schedule versus the percentage of vulnerabilities not remediated on schedule

Measure 17: System and Services Acquisition (SA) (program-level and system-level)

Field	Data
Measure ID	Service Acquisition Contract Measure 1 (or a unique identifier to be filled out by the organization)
Goal	- *Strategic Goal:* Accelerate the development and use of an electronic information infrastructure. - *Information Security Goal:* Ensure third-party providers employ adequate security measures to protect information, applications, and/or services outsourced from the organization.
Measure	Percentage (%) of system and service acquisition contracts that include security requirements and/or specifications NIST SP 800-53 Control – SA-4: Acquisitions
Measure Type	Implementation
Formula	(Number of system and service acquisition contracts that include security requirements and specifications/total number of system and service acquisition contracts) *100
Target	This should be a high percentage defined by the organization.
Implementation Evidence	1. How many active service acquisition contracts does the organization have? _____ 2. How many active service acquisition contracts include security requirements and specifications (SA-4)? _____
Frequency	Collection Frequency: Organization-defined (example: quarterly) Reporting Frequency: Organization-defined (example: annually)
Responsible Parties	- Information Owner: Organization-defined (example: Contracting Officer) - Information Collector: Organization-defined (example: Contracting Officer's Technical Representative, System Owner) - Information Customer: Contracting Officer's Technical Representative, System Owner, Procurement Officer, Chief Information Officer (CIO), Information System Security Officer (ISSO), Senior Agency Information Security Officer (SAISO) (e.g., Chief Information Security Officer [CISO])
Data Source	Service acquisition contracts
Reporting Format	Pie chart comparing the percentage of system and service acquisition contracts that include security requirements and/or specifications versus the percentage of system and service acquisition contracts that do not include security requirements and/or specifications

Measure 18: System and Communications Protection (SC) (program-level)

Field	Data
Measure ID	System and Communication Protection Measure 1 (or a unique identifier to be filled out by the organization)
Goal	- *Strategic Goal:* Accelerate the development and use of an electronic information infrastructure. - *Information Security Goal:* Allocate sufficient resources to adequately protect electronic information infrastructure.
Measure	Percentage of mobile computers and devices that perform all cryptographic operations using FIPS 140-2 validated cryptographic modules operating in approved modes of operation NIST SP 800-53 Control – SC-13: Use of Validated Cryptography
Measure Type	Implementation
Formula	(Number of mobile computers and devices that perform all cryptographic operations using FIPS 140-2 validated cryptographic modules operating in approved modes of operation/total number of mobile computers and devices) *100
Target	This should be a high percentage defined by the organization.

Implementation Evidence	1. How many mobile computers and devices are used in the organization (CM-8)? _____
	2. How many mobile computers and devices employ cryptography (CM-8)? _____
	   a. How many mobile computers and devices employ FIPS 140-2 validated encryption modules (SC-13)? _____
	   b. How many of those mobile computers and devices perform all cryptographic operations using FIPS 140-2 validated cryptographic modules operating in approved modes of operation (SC-13)? _____
	3. How many mobile computers and devices have cryptography implementation waivers (CM-8)? _____

Frequency	Collection Frequency: Organization-defined (example: quarterly) Reporting Frequency: Organization-defined (example: annually)
Responsible Parties	- Information Owner: Organization-defined (example: System Owners, Information System Security Officer [ISSO]) - Information Collector: Organization-defined (example: System Administrators, System Owners, Information System Security Officer [ISSO]) - Information Customer: Chief Information Officer (CIO), Information System Security Officer (ISSO), Senior Agency Information Security Officer (SAISO) (e.g., Chief Information Security Officer [CISO])
Data Source	System security plans
Reporting Format	Pie chart illustrating the number of mobile computers and devices that perform all cryptographic operations (including key generation) using FIPS 140-2 validated cryptographic modules operating in approved modes of operation as a percentage of the total number of mobile computers and devices

Measure 19: System and Information Integrity (SI) (program-level and system-level)

Field	Data
Measure ID	System and Information Integrity 1 (or a unique identifier to be filled out by the organization)
Goal	- *Strategic Goal:* Accelerate the development and use of an electronic information infrastructure. - *Information Security Goal:* Provide protection from malicious code at appropriate locations within organizational information systems, monitor information systems security alerts and advisories, and take appropriate actions in response.
Measure	Percentage (%) of operating system vulnerabilities for which patches have been applied or that have been otherwise mitigated NIST SP 800-53 Controls – SI-2: Flaw Remediation
Measure Type	Implementation and **Effectiveness**/Efficiency
Formula	(Number of vulnerabilities addressed in distributed alerts and advisories for which patches have been implemented, determined as non-applicable, or granted a waiver/total number of applicable vulnerabilities identified through alerts and advisories and through vulnerability scans) *100
Target	This should be a high percentage defined by the organization.
Implementation Evidence	1. Does the organization distribute alerts and advisories (SI-5)? ☐ Yes ☐ No 2. How many vulnerabilities were identified by analyzing distributed alerts and advisories (SI-5)? _____ 3. How many vulnerabilities were identified through vulnerability scans (RA-5)? _____ 4. How many patches or work-arounds were implemented to address identified vulnerabilities (SI-2)? _____ 5. How many vulnerabilities were determined to be non-applicable (SI-2)? _____ 6. How many waivers have been granted for weaknesses that could not be remediated by implementing patches or work-arounds? _____
Frequency	Collection Frequency: Organization-defined (example: weekly) Reporting Frequency: Organization-defined (example: monthly)
Responsible Parties	- Information Owner: Organization-defined (example: Computer Security Incident Response Team [CSIRT]) - Information Collector: Organization-defined (example: Information System Security Officer [ISSO], System Owners) - Information Customer: Chief Information Officer (CIO), Information System Security Officer (ISSO), Senior Agency Information Security Officer (SAISO) (e.g., Chief Information Security Officer [CISO])
Data Source	Vulnerability scans, POA&Ms, repositories of alerts and advisories, risk assessments

Field	Data
Reporting Format	Stacked bar chart with total number of applicable vulnerabilities composed of percentages of number of vulnerabilities addressed in distributed alerts and advisories for which patches have been determined as non-applicable, have been implemented, have had a waiver granted, or other

Appendix B: ACRONYMS

AC	Access Control
AO	Authorizing Official
AT	Awareness and Training
AU	Audit and Accountability
C&A	Certification and Accreditation
CFO	Chief Financial Officer
CIO	Chief Information Officer
CISO	Chief Information Security Officer
CM	Configuration Management
COTS	Commercial Off-The-Shelf
CP	Contingency Planning
CPIC	Capital Planning and Investment Control
CSIRT	Computer Security Incident Response Team
FEA	Federal Enterprise Architecture
FIPS	Federal Information Processing Standards
FISCAM	Federal Information System Controls Audit Manual
FISMA	Federal Information Security Management Act
FY	Fiscal Year
GAO	Government Accountability Office
GOTS	Government Off-The-Shelf
GPEA	Government Paperwork Elimination Act
GPRA	Government Performance and Results Act
ID	Identification
IG	Inspector General
IR	Incident Response
ISSEA	International Systems Security Engineering Association
ISSO	Information System Security Officer
ITL	Information Technology Laboratory
MP	Media Protection
NIST	National Institute of Standards and Technology
OMB	Office of Management and Budget
PE	Physical and Environmental
PL	Planning
POA&M	Plan of Action and Milestones
PRM	Performance Reference Model
PS	Physical Security
RA	Risk Assessment
SA	System and Services Acquisition
SAISO	Senior Agency Information Security Officer
SC	System and Communications Protection
SDLC	System Development Life Cycle
SI	System and Information Integrity
SP	Special Publication
USC	United States Code

US-CERT	United States Computer Emergency Readiness Team
XML	Extensible Markup Language

Appendix C: REFERENCES

Bartol N., Givans N., *Measuring the "Goodness" of Security*, 2nd International Systems Security Engineering Association (ISSEA) Conference Proceedings, February 2001.

Bartol N., *Information Security Performance Measurement: Live,* 3rd ISSEA Conference Proceedings, March 2002.

Clinger-Cohen Act of 1996 (formerly known as the Information Technology Management Reform Act), February 10, 1996.

E-Government Act, Title III—Federal Information Security Management Act (P.L 107-347), December 2002.

Federal Information Processing Standards (FIPS) 199, *Standards for Security Categorization of Federal Information and Information Systems,* February 2004.

Federal Information Processing Standards (FIPS) 200, *Minimum Security Requirements for Federal Information and Information Systems,* March 2006.

Floyd D. Spence National Defense Authorization Act for Fiscal Year 2001 (P.L. 106-398).

General Accounting Office, *Federal Information System Controls Audit Manual (FISCAM),* GAO/AIMD-12.19.6, January 1996.

Government Performance and Results Act of 1993 (PL. 103-62).

National Institute of Standards and Technology Interagency Report 7298, *Glossary of Key Information Security Terms,* April, 2006.

National Institute of Standards and Technology Special Publication 800-18, *Guide for Developing Security Plans and Information Technology Systems,* February 2006.

National Institute of Standards and Technology Special Publication 800-30, *Risk Management Guide for Information Technology Systems,* June 2001.

National Institute of Standards and Technology Special Publication 800-37, *Guide for the Security Certification and Accreditation of Federal Information Systems*, May 2004.

National Institute of Standards and Technology Special Publication 800-53, *Recommended Security Controls for Federal Information Systems*, December 2007..

National Institute of Standards and Technology Special Publication 800-53A, *Guide for Assessing the Security Controls in Federal Information Systems*, June 2008.

National Institute of Standards and Technology Special Publication 800-65, *Integrating Security into the Capital Planning and Investment Control Process*, January 2005.

National Institute of Standards and Technology Special Publication 800-100, *Information Security Handbook: A Guide for Managers*, October 2006.

Office of Management and Budget, "Security of Federal Automated Information Resources," Appendix III to OMB Circular A-130, *Management of Federal Information Resources*, February 8, 1996.

Office of Management and Budget Circular A-11, *Preparation, Submission, and Execution of the Budget, Part 6, Preparation and Submission of Strategic Plans, Annual Performance Plans, and Annual Program Performance Reports* (updated annually).

Appendix D: SPECIFICATIONS FOR MINIMUM SECURITY REQUIREMENTS[14]

- **Access Control (AC):** Organizations must limit information system access to authorized users, processes acting on behalf of authorized users, or devices (including other information systems), and to the types of transactions and functions that authorized users are permitted to exercise.

- **Awareness and Training (AT):** Organizations must: (i) ensure that managers and users of organizational information systems are made aware of the information security risks associated with their activities and of the applicable laws, Executive orders, directives, policies, standards, instructions, regulations, or procedures related to the information security of organizational information systems; and (ii) ensure that organizational personnel are adequately trained to carry out their assigned information security-related duties and responsibilities.

- **Audit and Accountability (AU):** Organizations must: (i) create, protect, and retain information system audit records to the extent needed to enable the monitoring, analysis, investigation, and reporting of unlawful, unauthorized, or inappropriate information system activity; and (ii) ensure that the actions of individual information system users can be uniquely traced to those users so that they can be held accountable for their actions.

- **Certification, Accreditation, and Security Assessments (CA):** Organizations must: (i) periodically assess the security controls in organizational information systems to determine if the controls are effective in their application; (ii) develop and implement plans of action designed to correct deficiencies and reduce or eliminate vulnerabilities in organizational information systems; (iii) authorize the operation of organizational information systems and any associated information system connections; and (iv) monitor information system security controls on an ongoing basis to ensure the continued effectiveness of the controls.

- **Configuration Management (CM):** Organizations must: (i) establish and maintain baseline configurations and inventories of organizational information systems (including hardware, software, firmware, and documentation) throughout the respective information system development life cycles; and (ii) establish and enforce information security configuration settings for information technology products employed in organizational information systems.

- **Contingency Planning (CP):** Organizations must establish, maintain, and effectively implement plans for emergency response, backup operations, and post-disaster recovery for organizational information systems to ensure the availability of critical information resources and continuity of operations in emergency situations.

- **Identification and Authentication (IA):** Organizations must identify information system users, processes acting on behalf of users, or devices and authenticate (or verify)

---

[14] FIPS 200, *Minimum Security Requirements for Federal Information and Information Systems*, March 2006.

the identities of those users, processes, or devices, as a prerequisite to allowing access to organizational information systems.

- **Incident Response (IR):** Organizations must: (i) establish an operational incident handling capability for organizational information systems that includes adequate preparation, detection, analysis, containment, recovery, and user response activities; and (ii) track, document, and report incidents to appropriate organizational officials and/or authorities.

- **Maintenance (MA):** Organizations must: (i) perform periodic and timely maintenance on organizational information systems; and (ii) provide effective controls on the tools, techniques, mechanisms, and personnel used to conduct information system maintenance.

- **Media Protection (MP):** Organizations must: (i) protect information system media, both paper and digital; (ii) limit access to information on information system media to authorized users; and (iii) sanitize or destroy information system media before disposal or release for reuse.

- **Physical and Environmental Protection (PE):** Organizations must: (i) limit physical access to information systems, equipment, and the respective operating environments to authorized individuals; (ii) protect the physical plant and support infrastructure for information systems; (iii) provide supporting utilities for information systems; (iv) protect information systems against environmental hazards; and (v) provide appropriate environmental controls in facilities containing information systems.

- **Planning (PL):** Organizations must develop, document, periodically update, and implement system security plans for organizational information systems that describe the security controls in place or planned for the information systems and the rules of behavior for individuals accessing the information systems.

- **Personnel Security (PS):** Organizations must: (i) ensure that individuals occupying positions of responsibility within organizations (including third-party service providers) are trustworthy and meet established information security criteria for those positions; (ii) ensure that organizational information and information systems are protected during personnel actions such as terminations and transfers; and (iii) employ formal sanctions for personnel failing to comply with organizational information security policies and procedures.

- **Risk Assessment (RA):** Organizations must periodically assess the risk to organizational operations (including mission, functions, image, or reputation), organizational assets, and individuals resulting from the operation of organizational information systems and the associated processing, storage, or transmission of organizational information.

- **System and Services Acquisition (SA):** Organizations must: (i) allocate sufficient resources to adequately protect organizational information systems; (ii) employ information system development life cycle processes that incorporate information security considerations; (iii) employ software usage and installation restrictions; and (iv) ensure that third-party providers employ adequate information security measures to protect information, applications, and/or services outsourced from the organization.

- **System and Communications Protection (SC):** Organizations must: (i) monitor, control, and protect organizational communications (i.e., information transmitted or received by organizational information systems) at the external boundaries and key internal boundaries of the information systems; and (ii) employ architectural designs, software development techniques, and information systems engineering principles that promote effective information security within organizational information systems.

- **System and Information Integrity (SI):** Organizations must: (i) identify, report, and correct information and information system flaws in a timely manner; (ii) provide protection from malicious code at appropriate locations within organizational information systems; and (iii) monitor information system security alerts and advisories and take appropriate actions in response.

www.ingramcontent.com/pod-product-compliance
Lightning Source LLC
Chambersburg PA
CBHW081842170526
45167CB00007B/2881